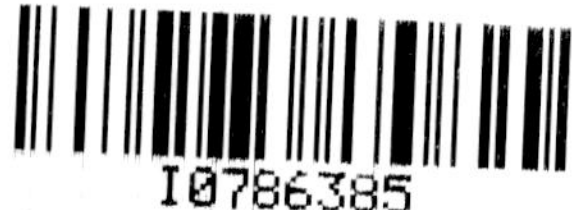

Mindfulness Coloring Book

Copyright: Published in the United States by Peter Raymond
Published August 2018
ISBN-13: 978-1724777416
ISBN-10: 1724777416

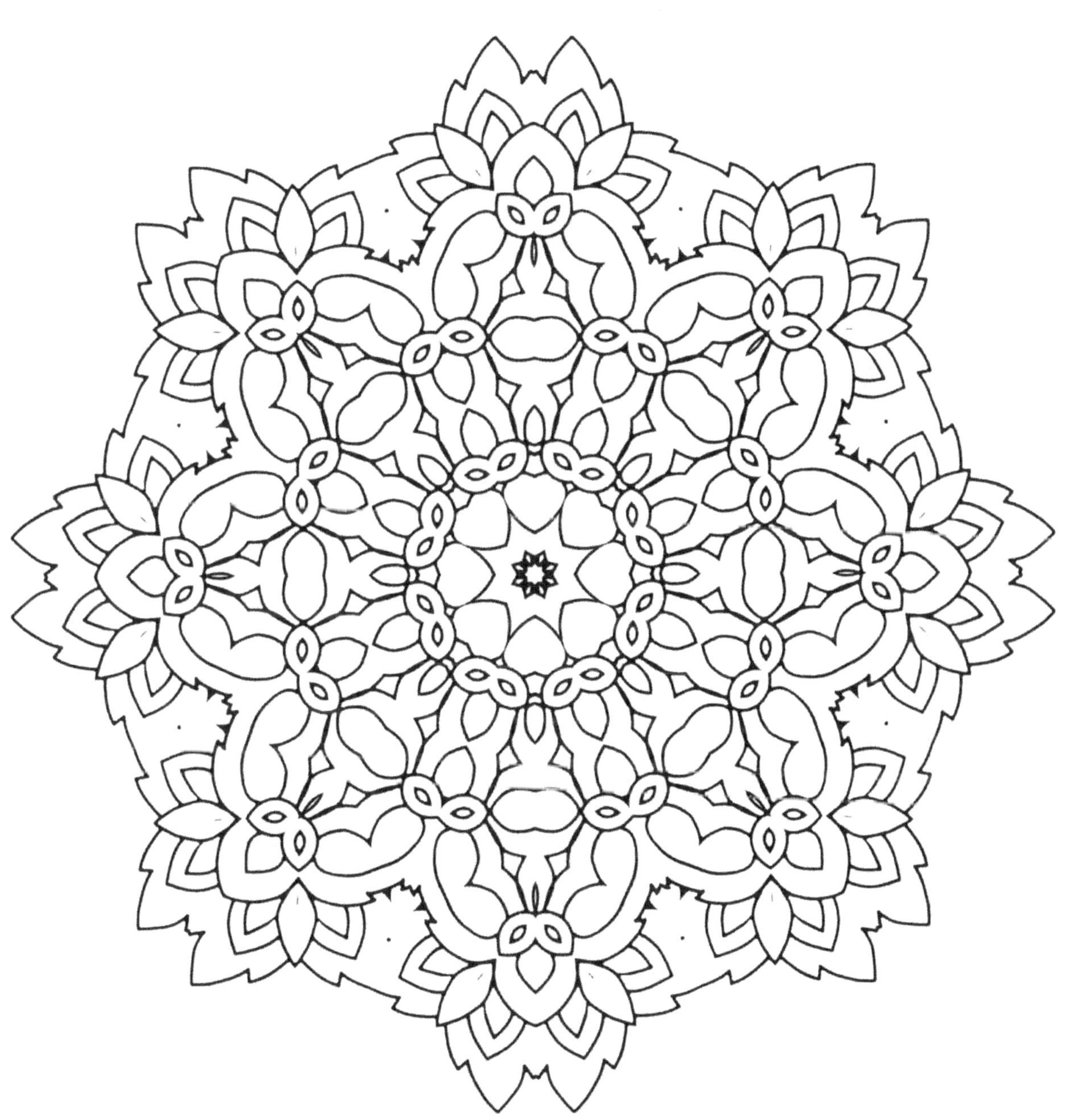

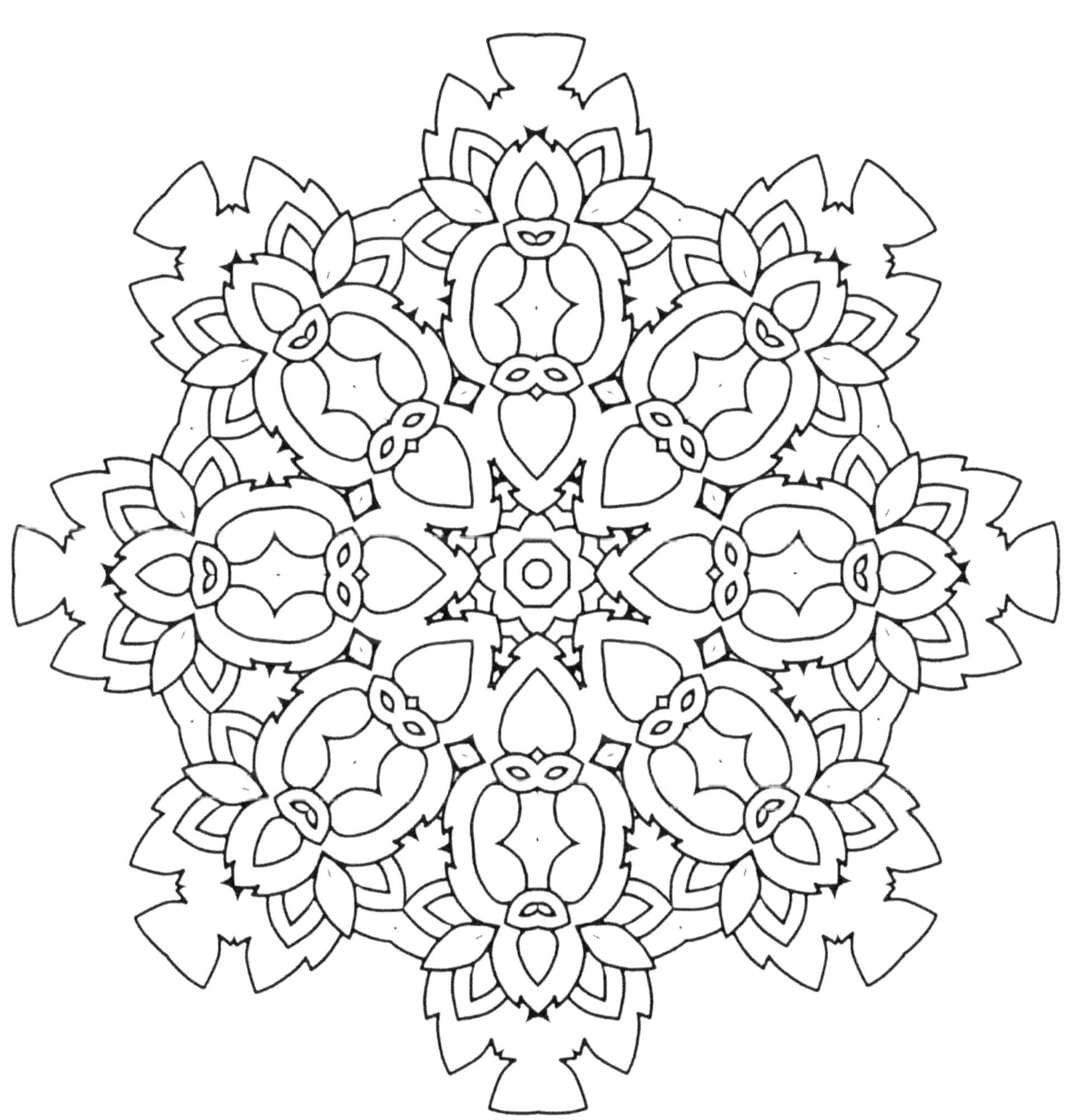

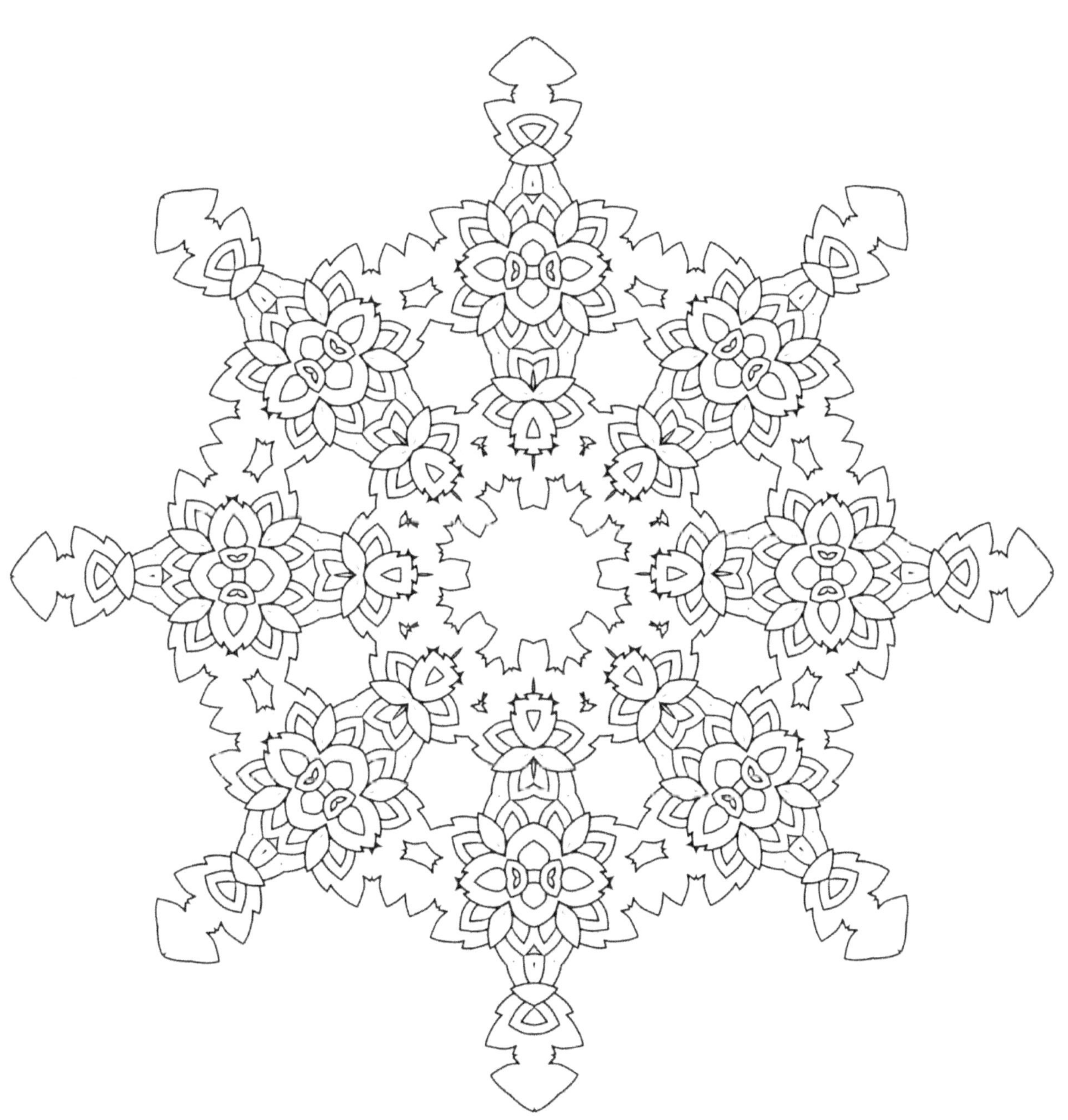

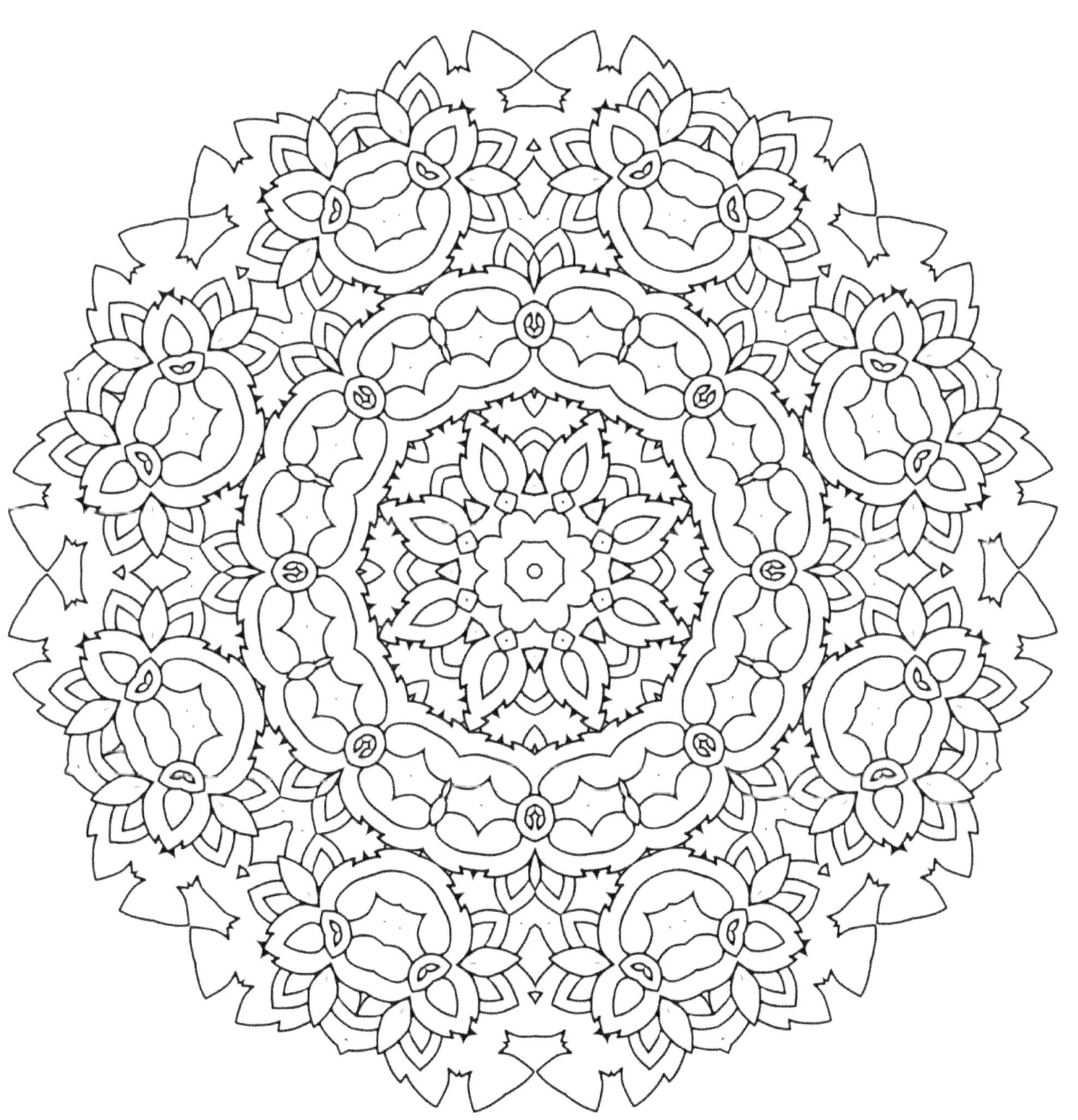

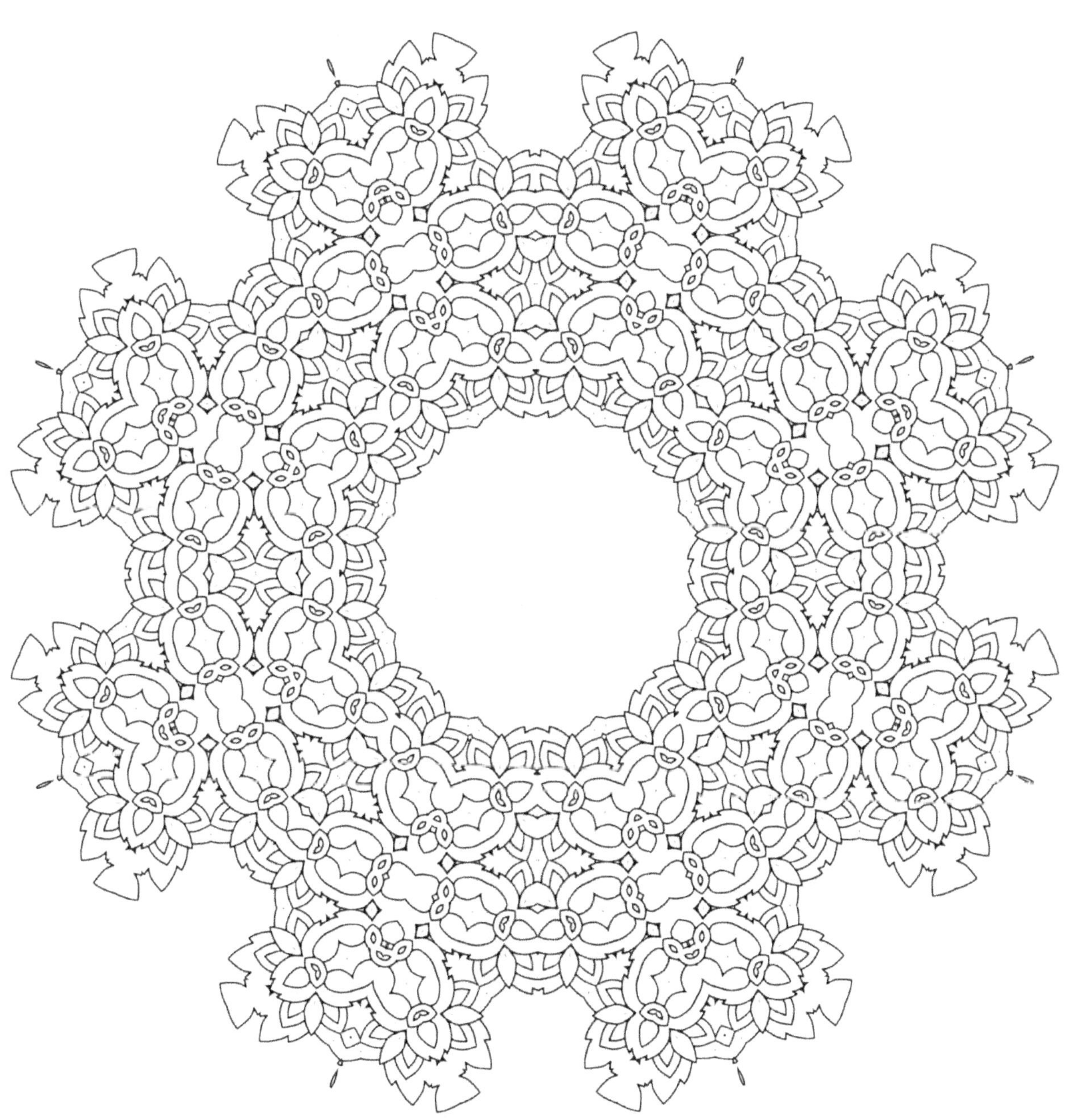

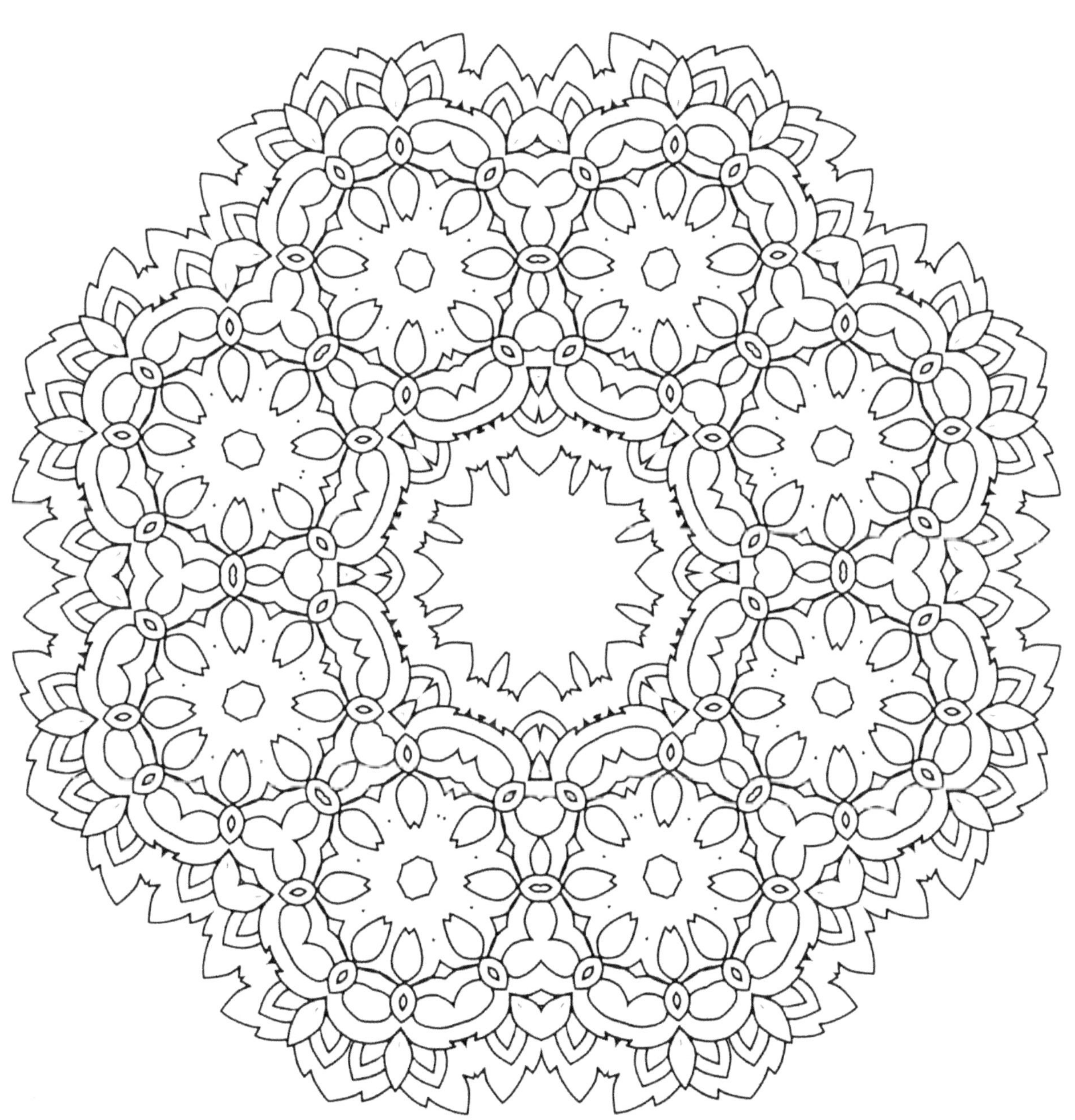

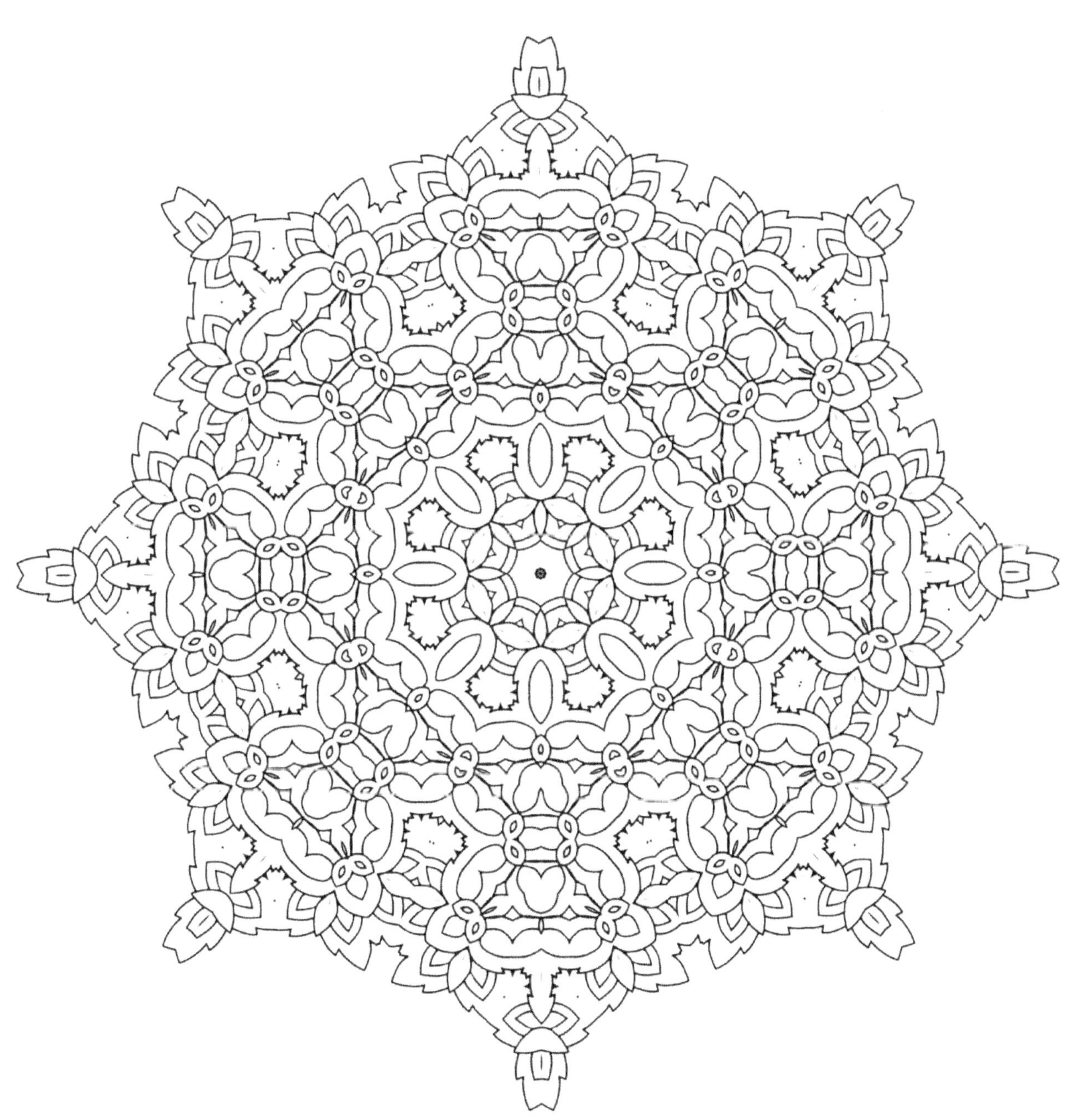

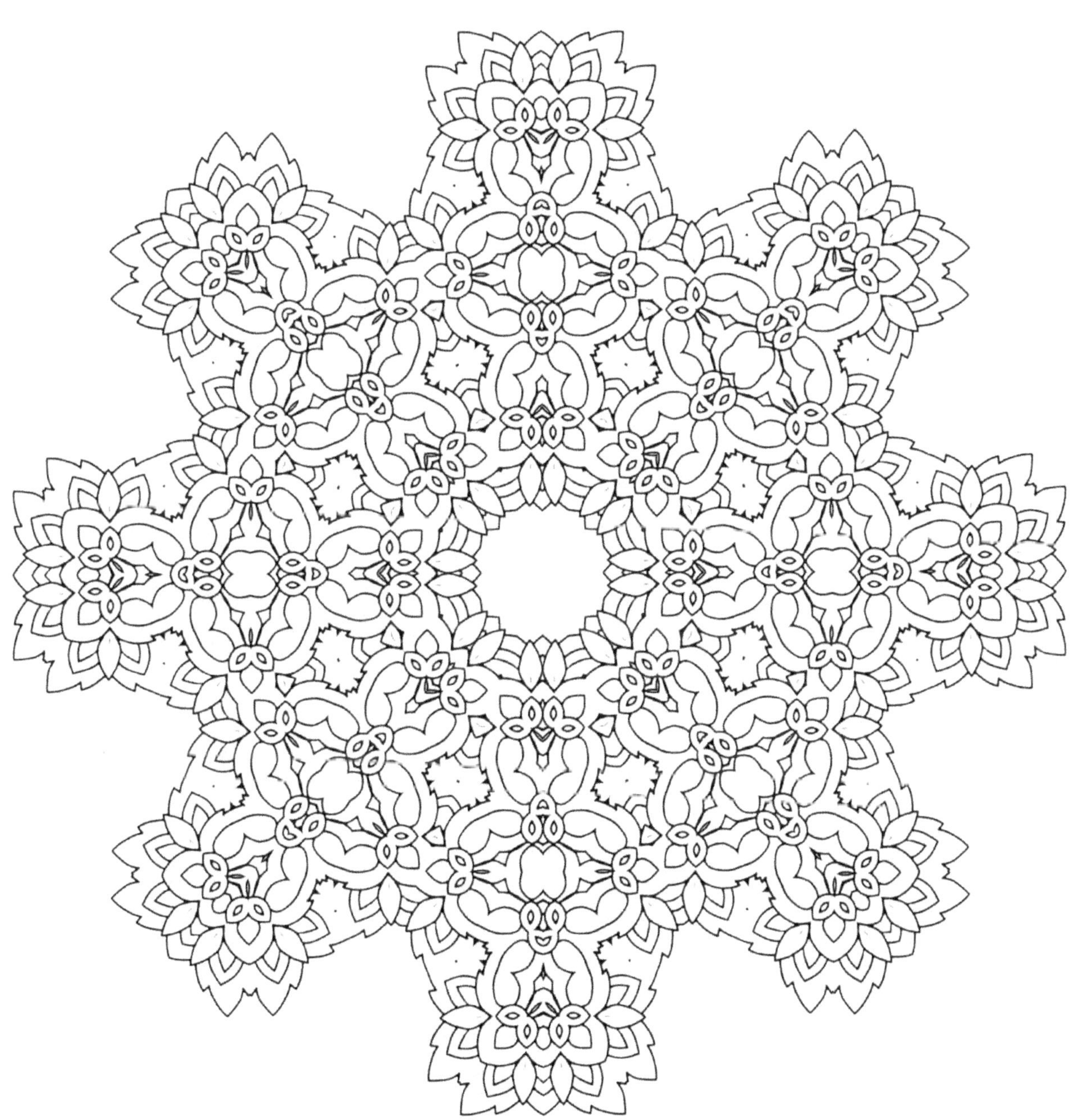

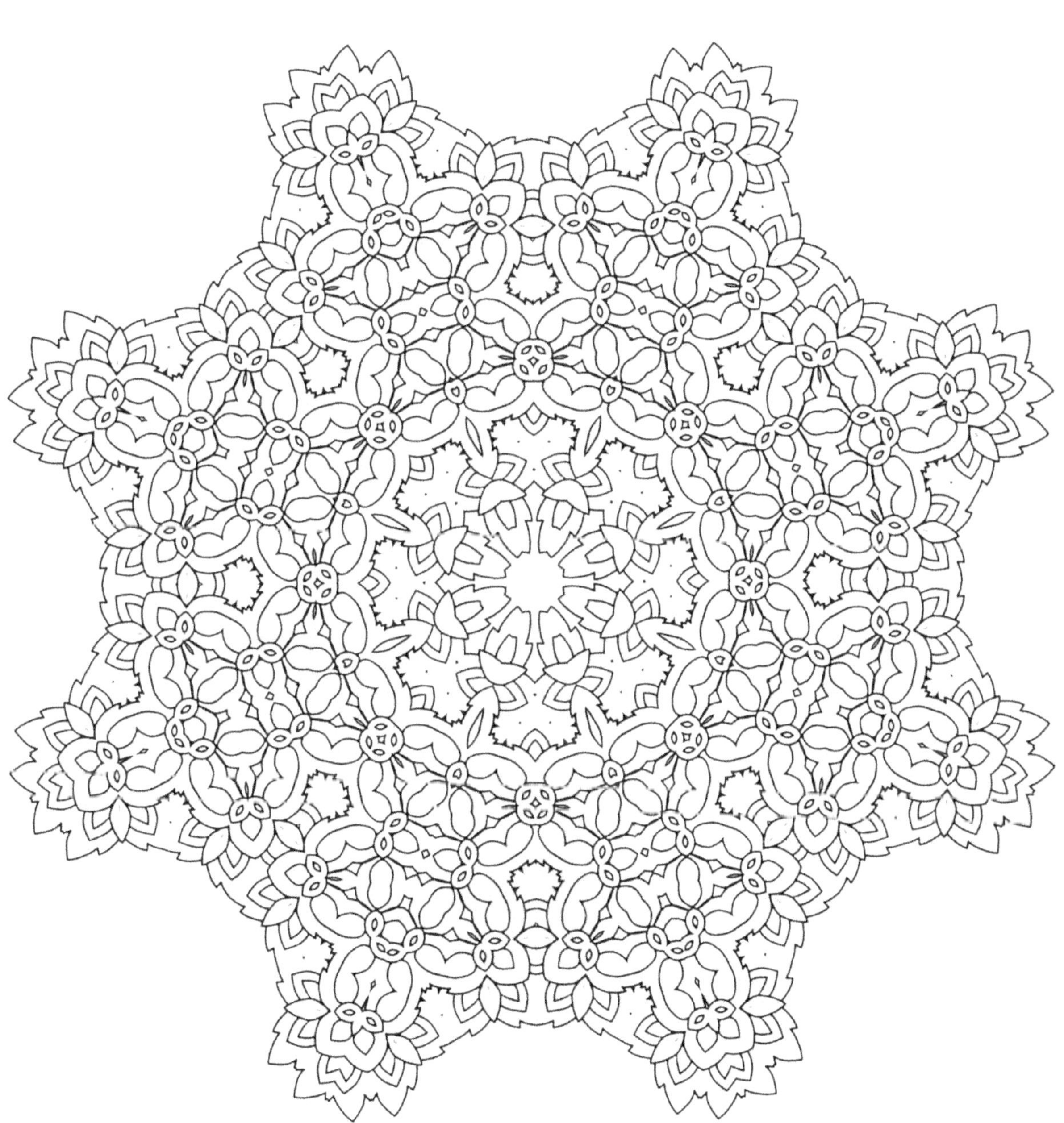

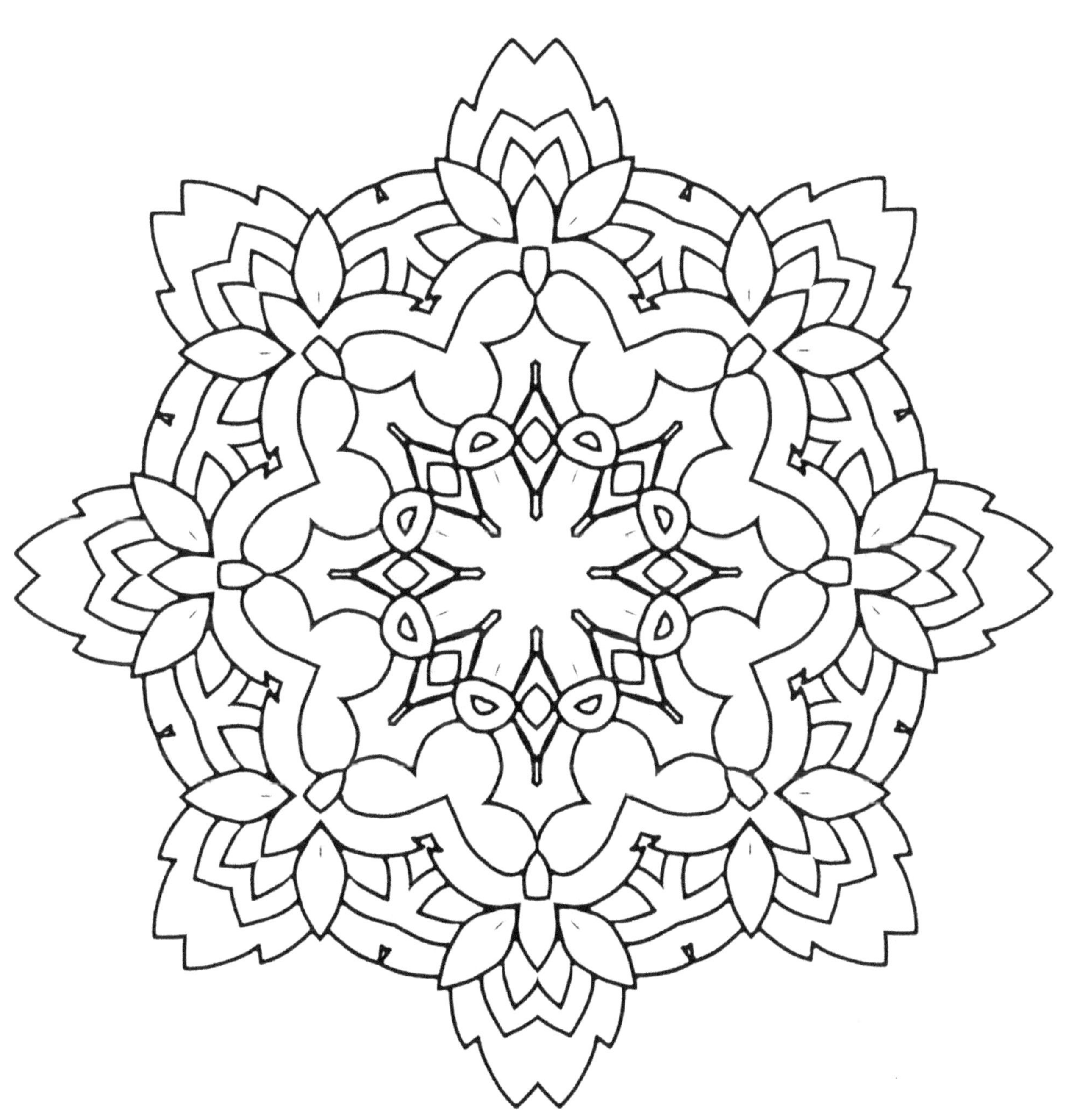

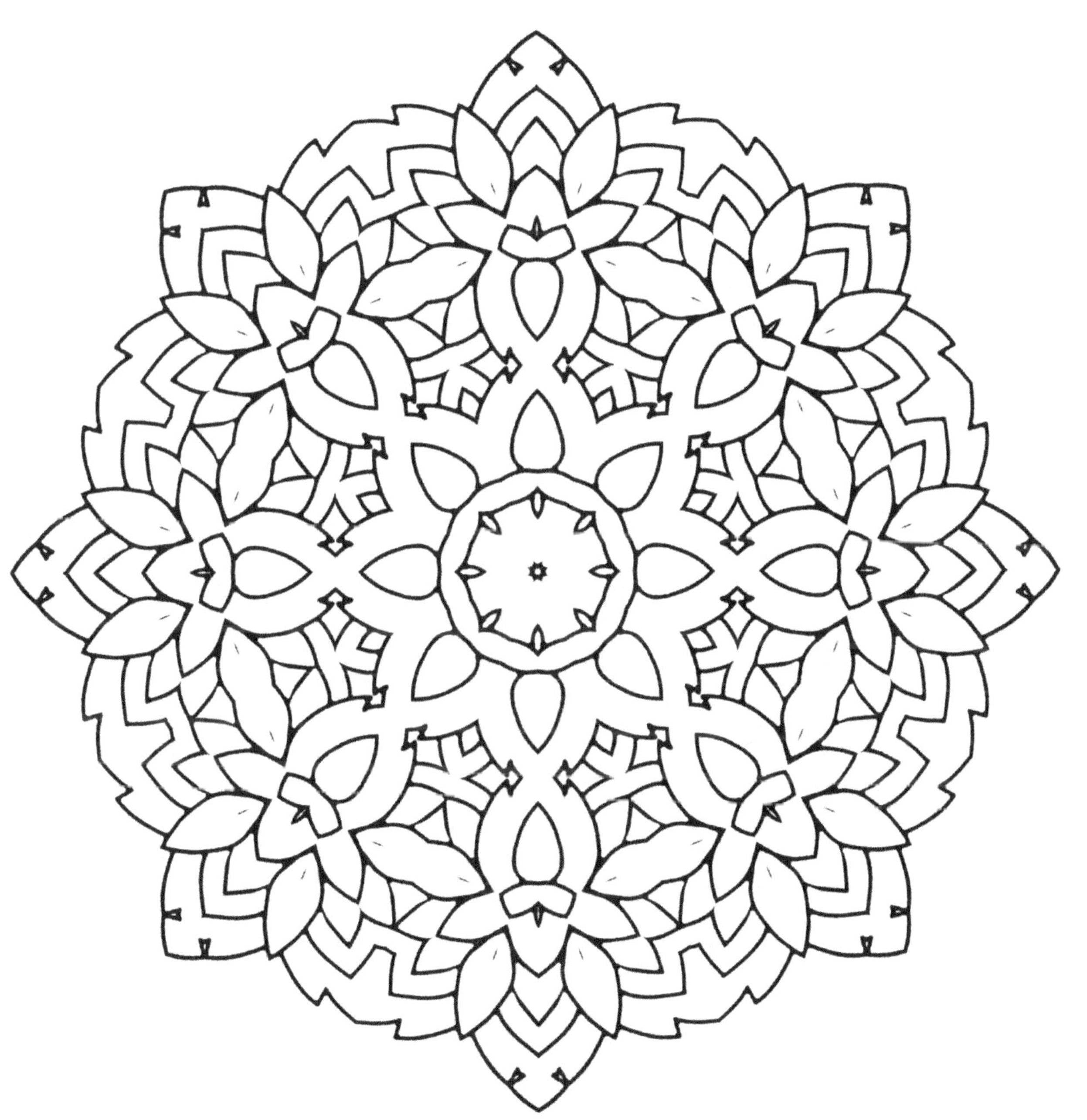

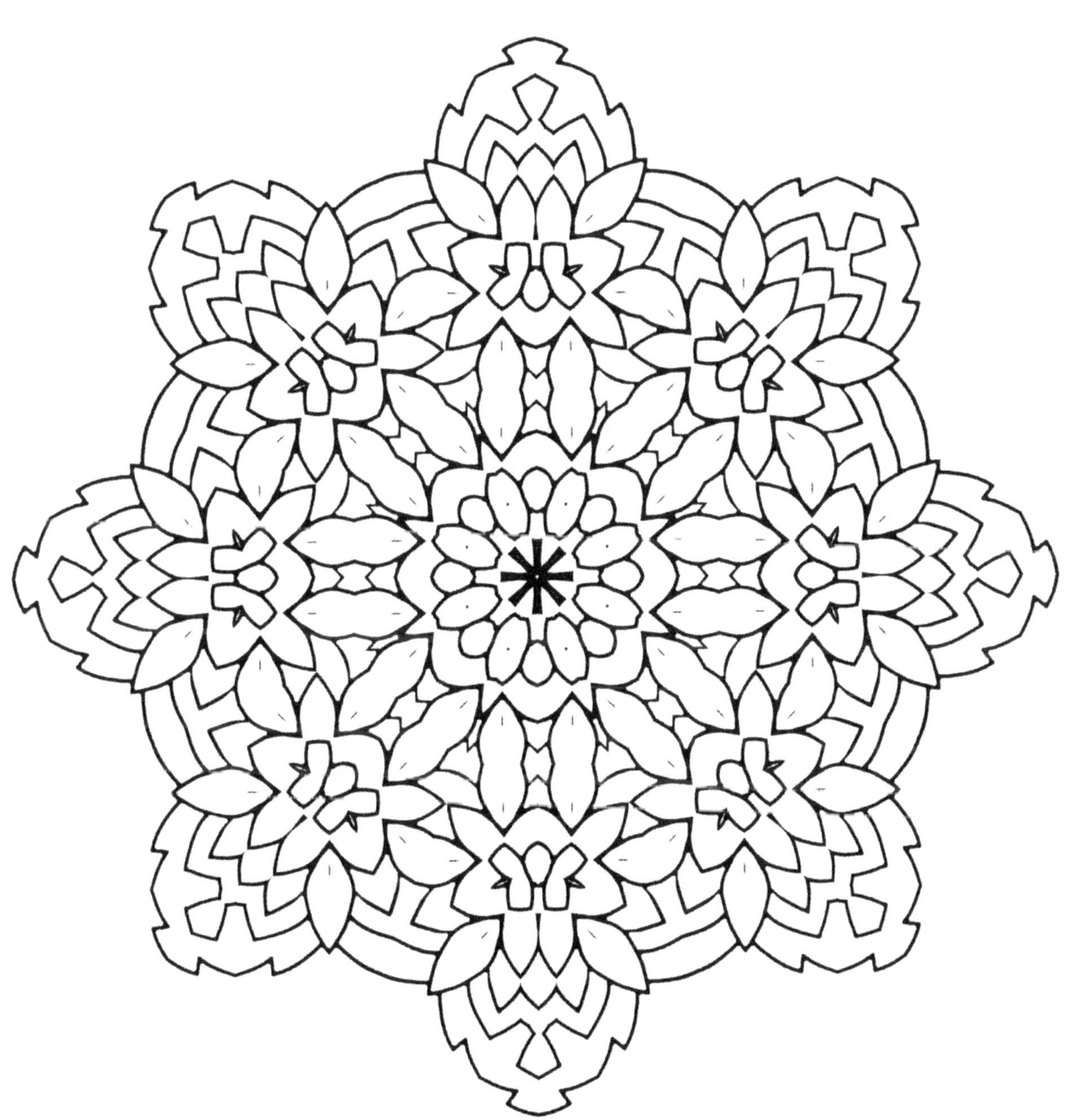

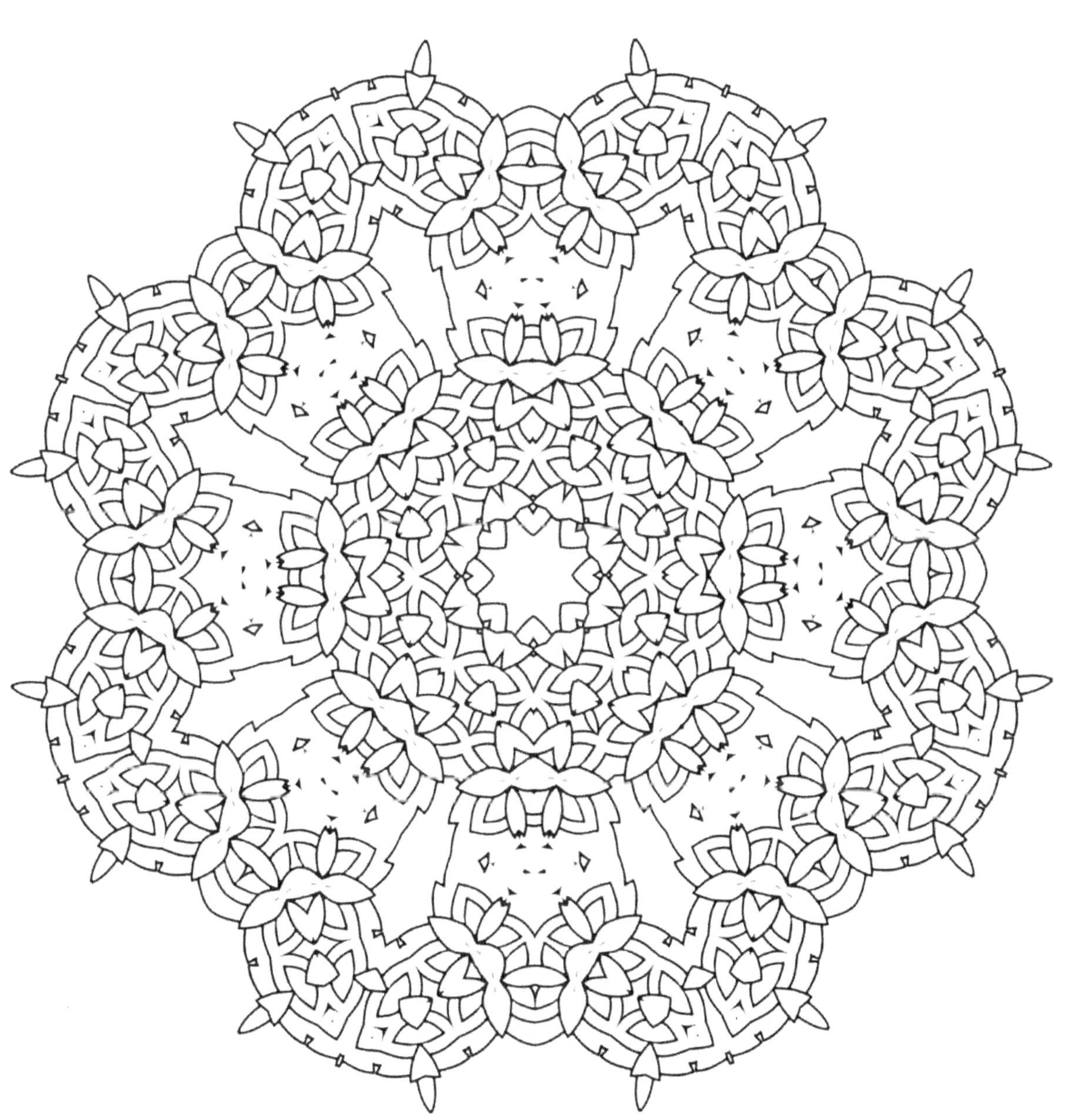

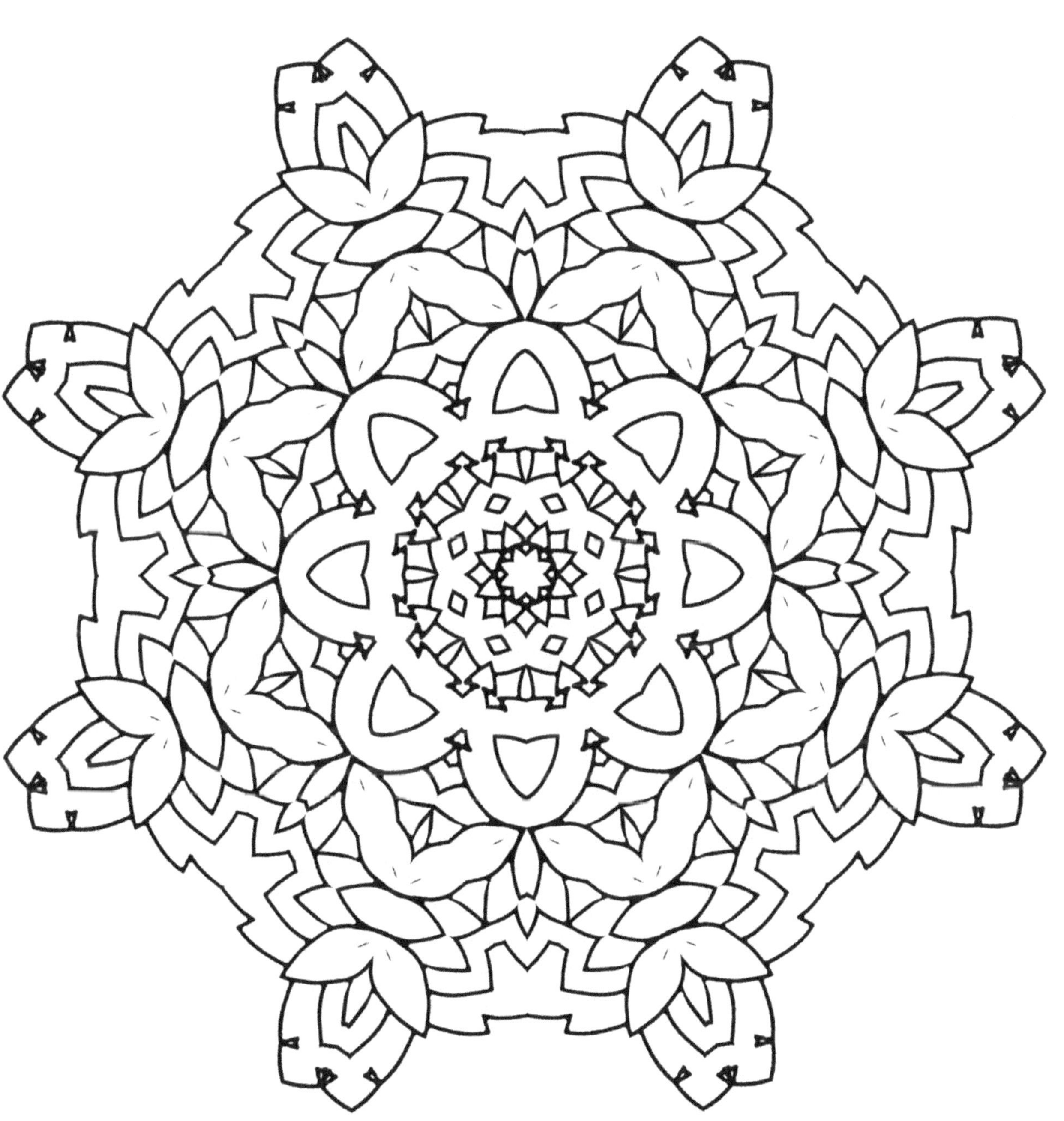

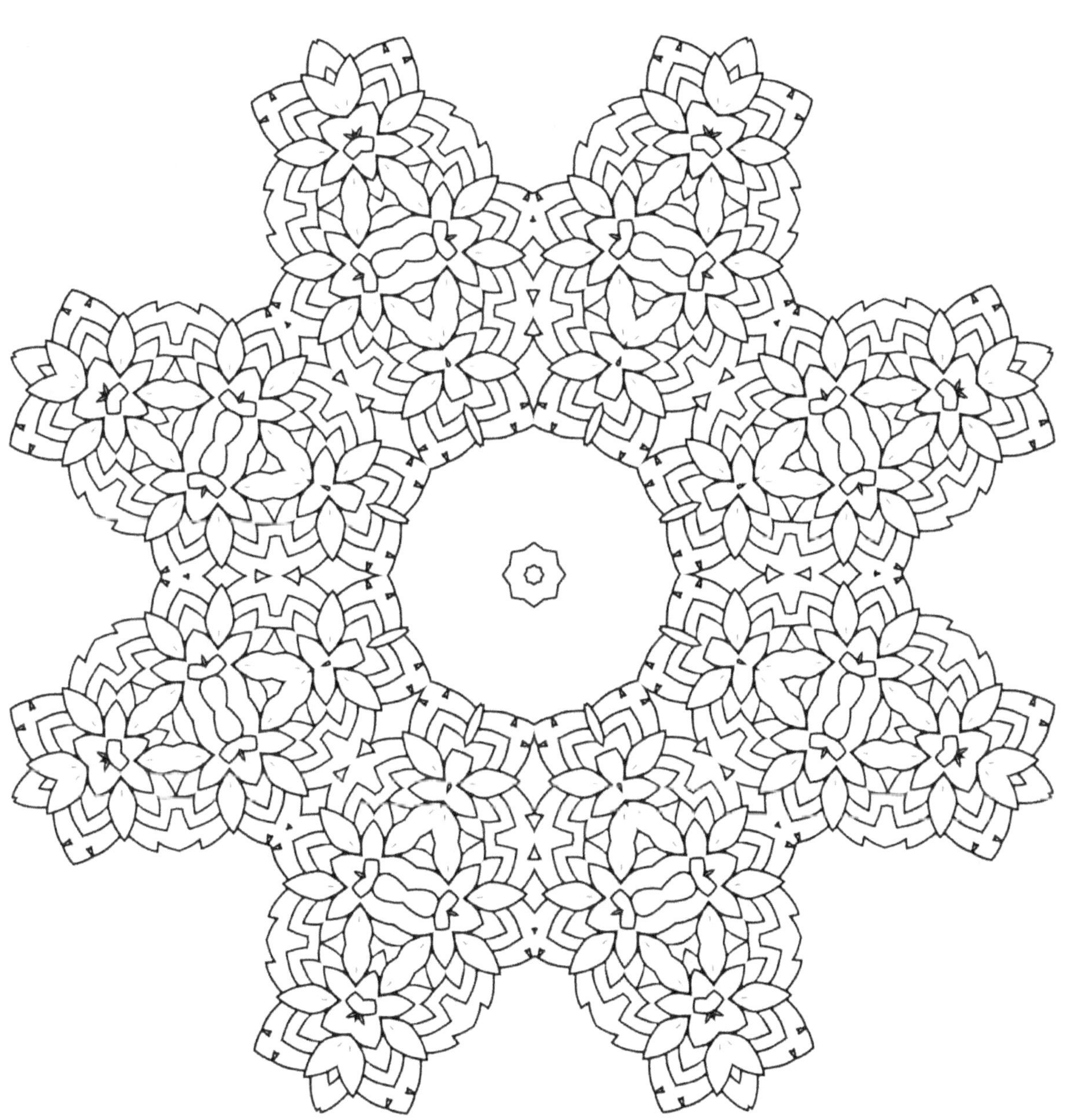

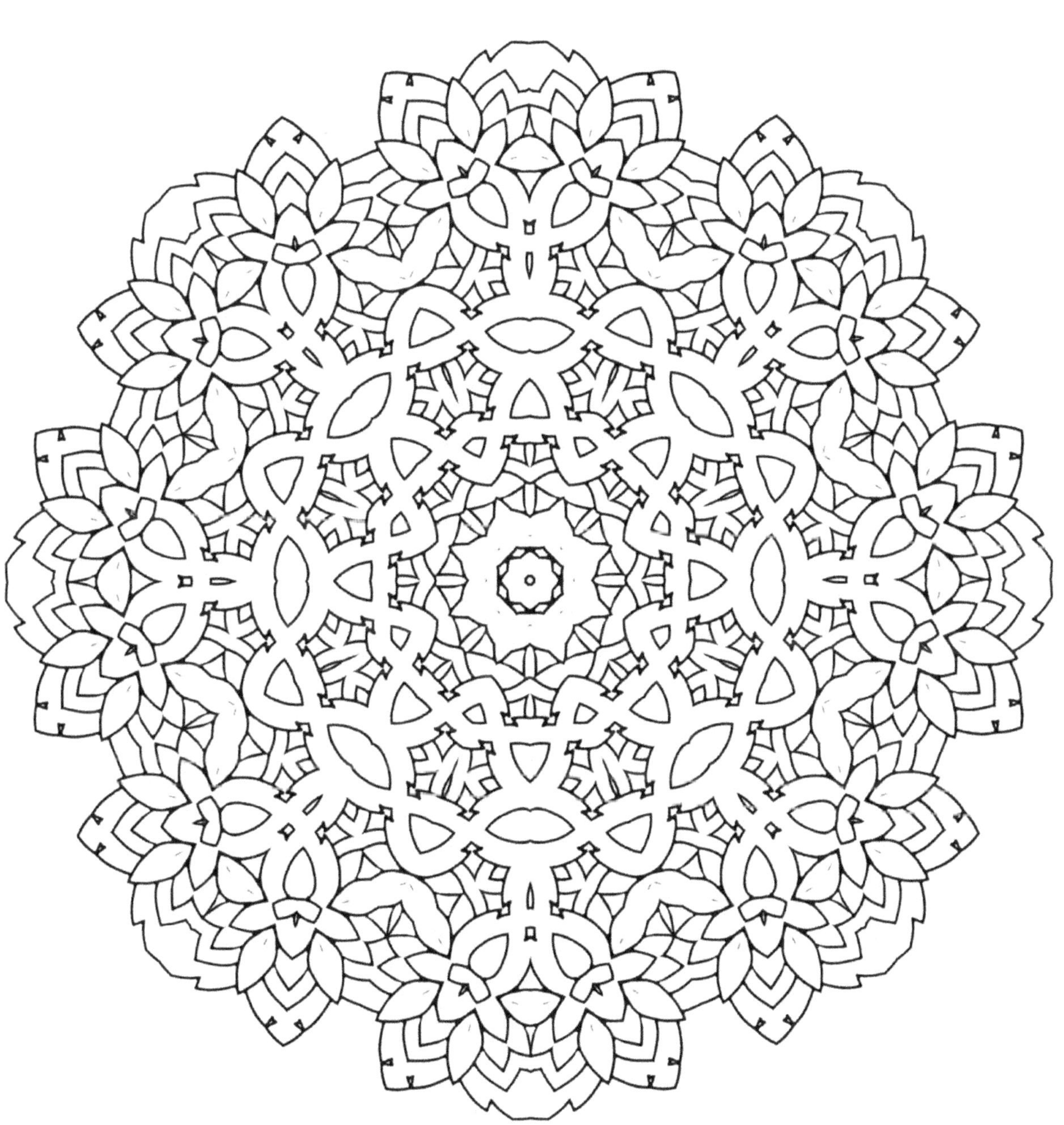

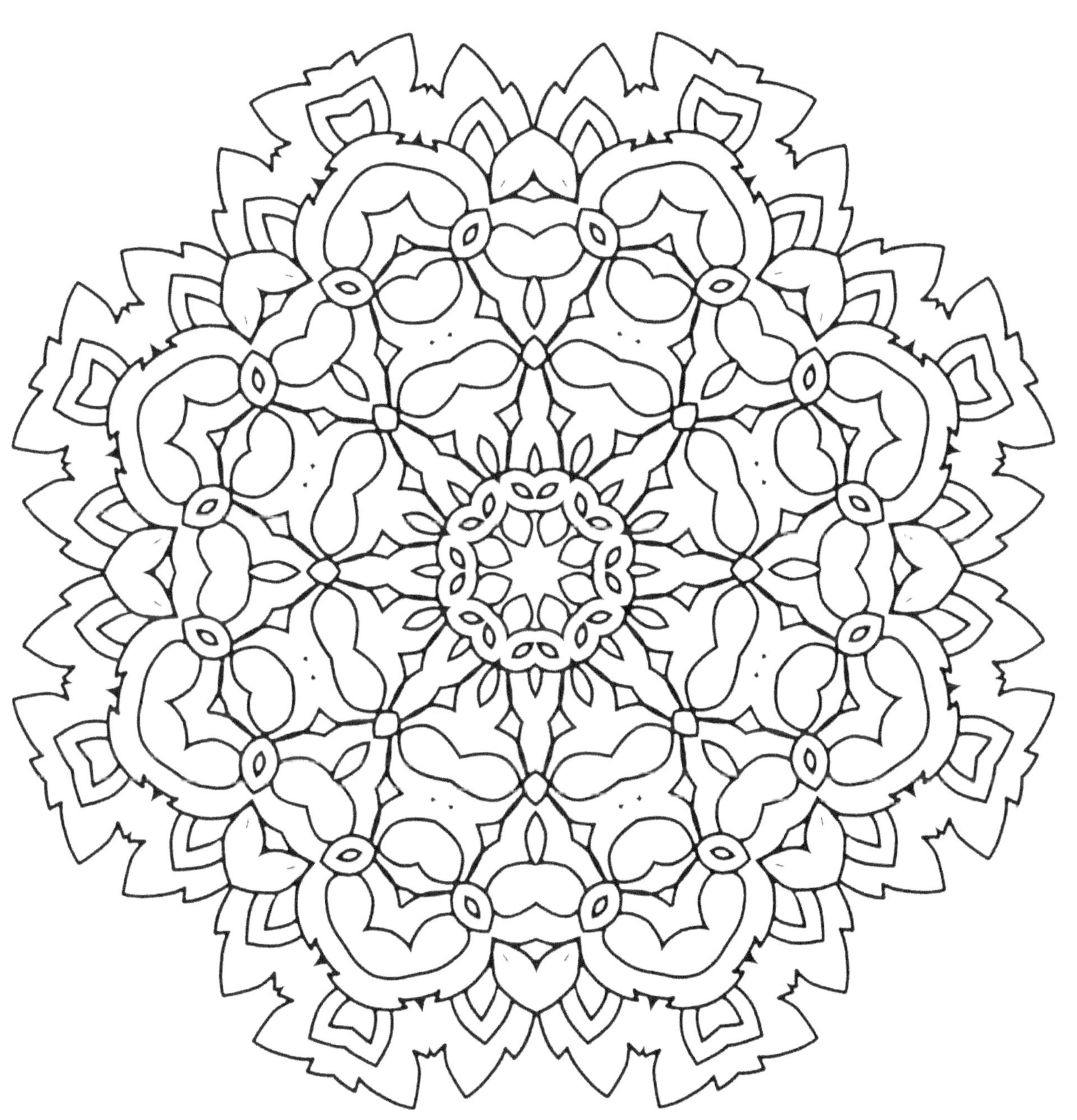

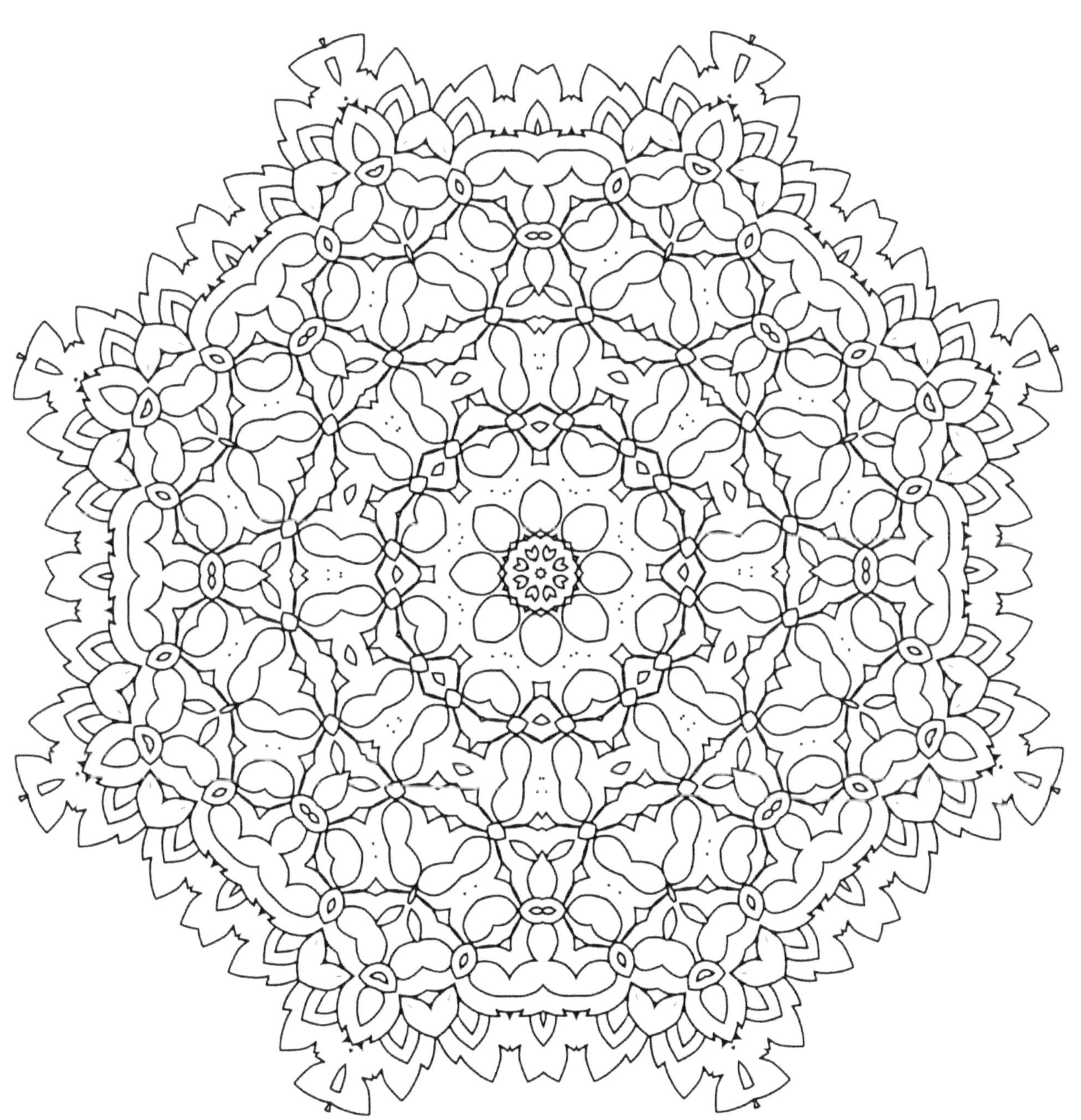

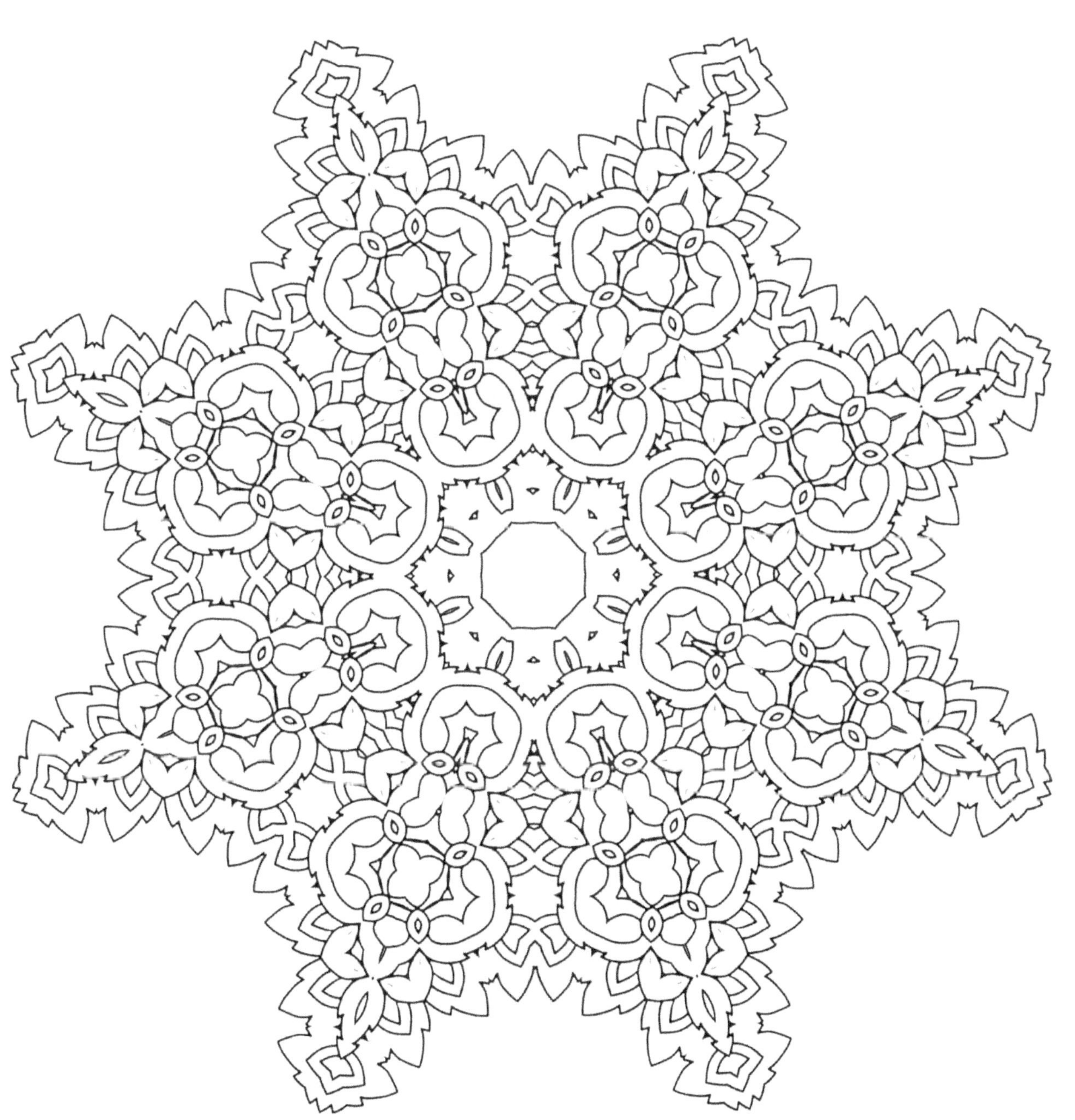

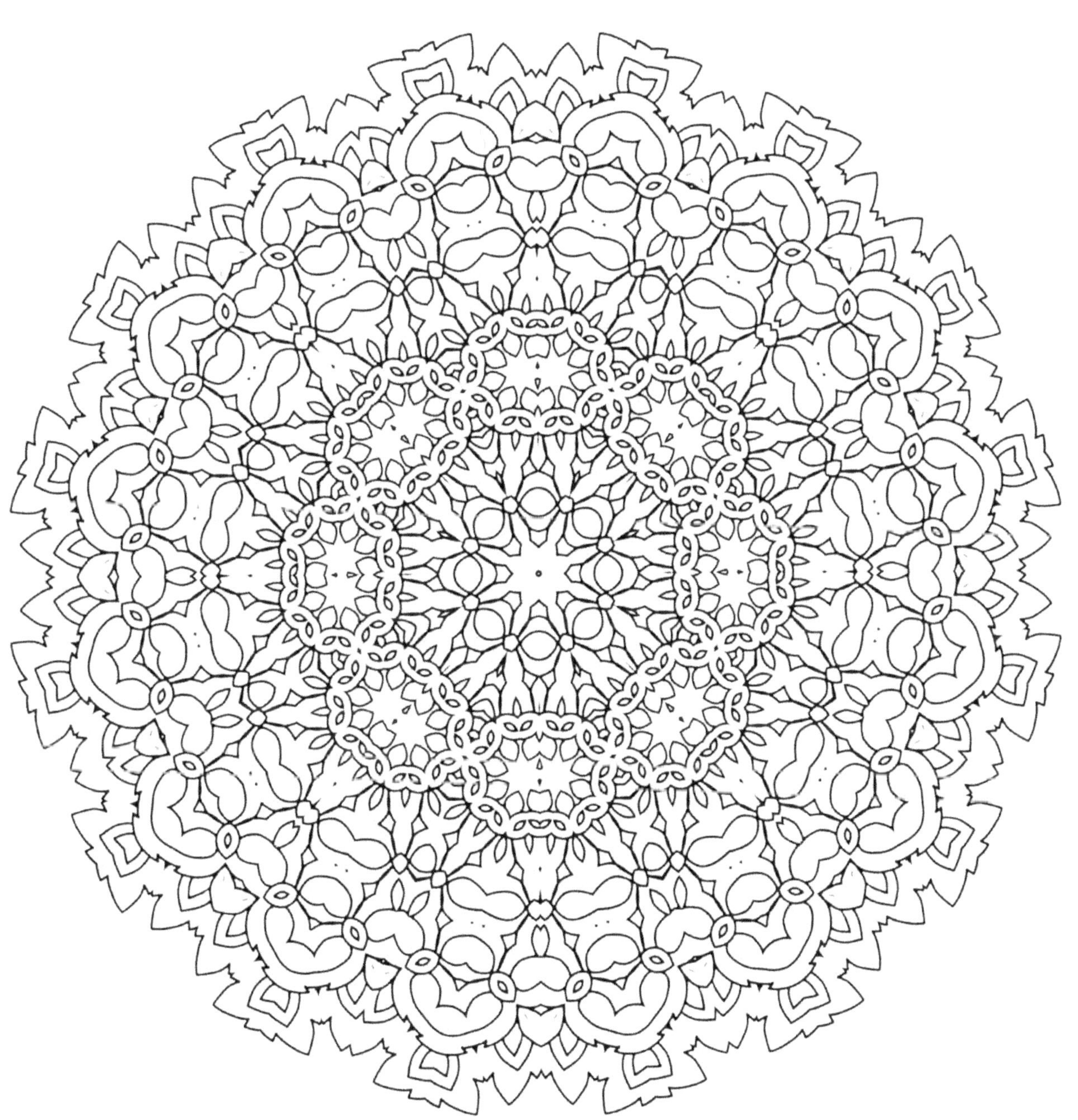

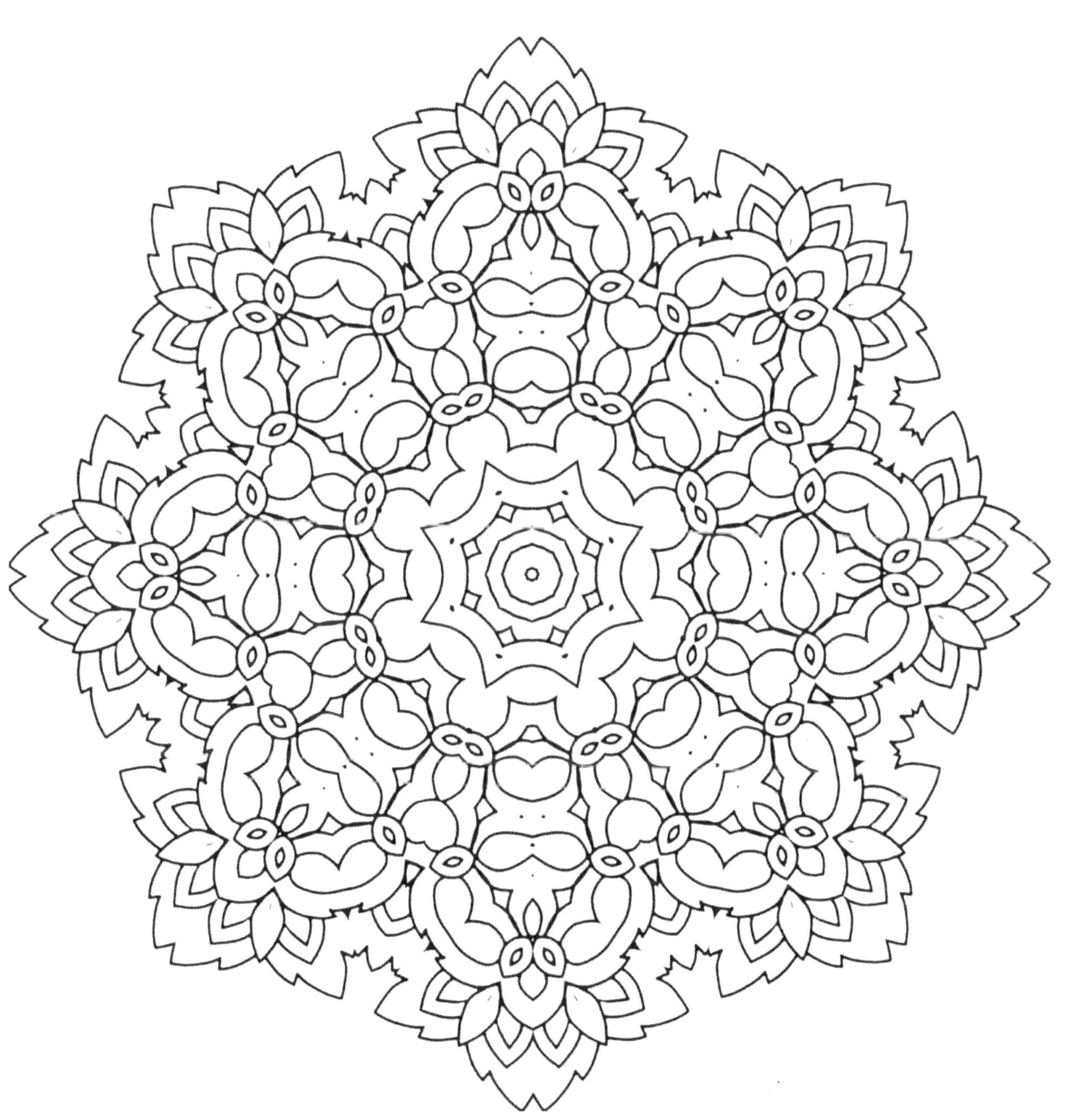

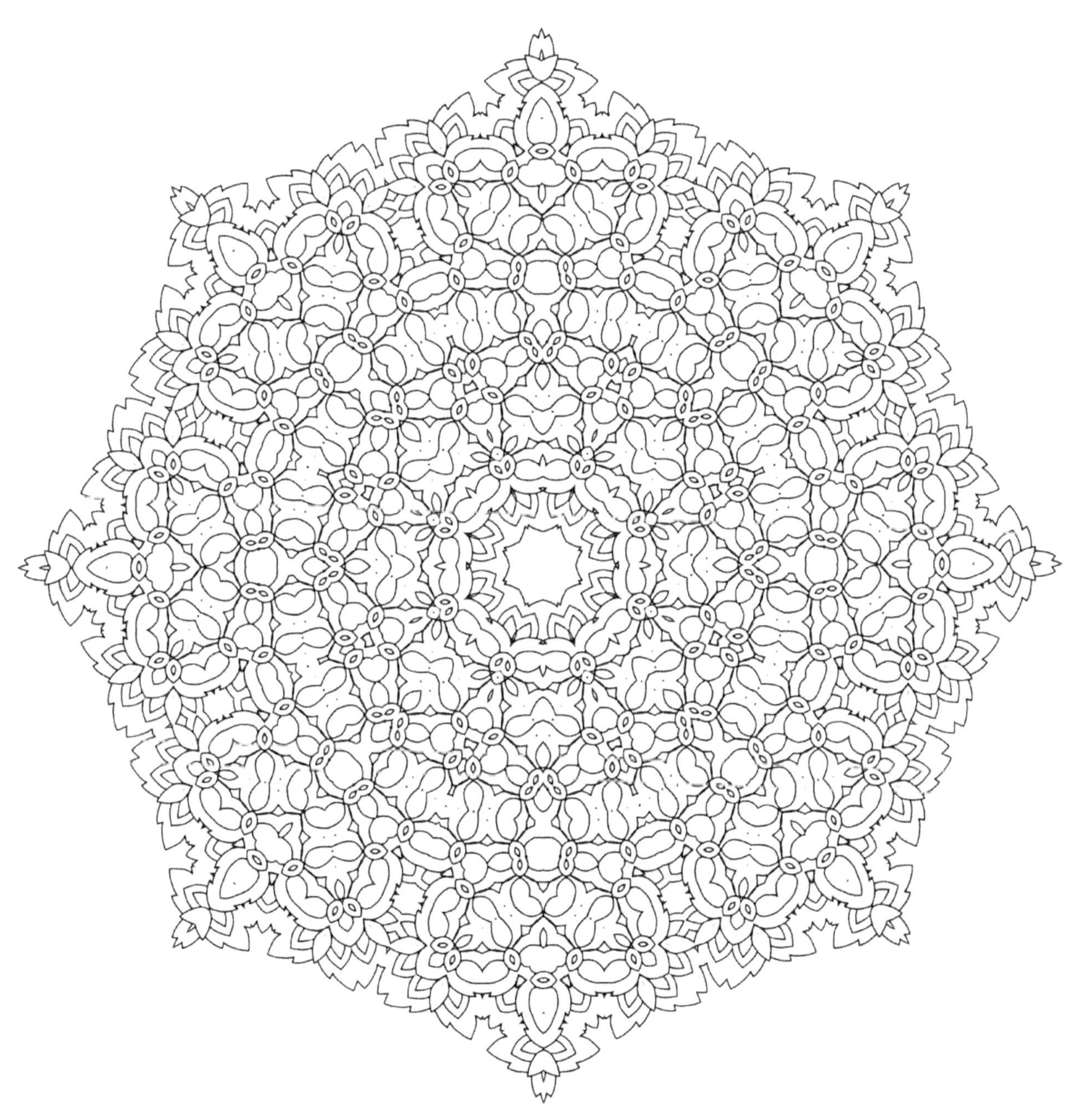

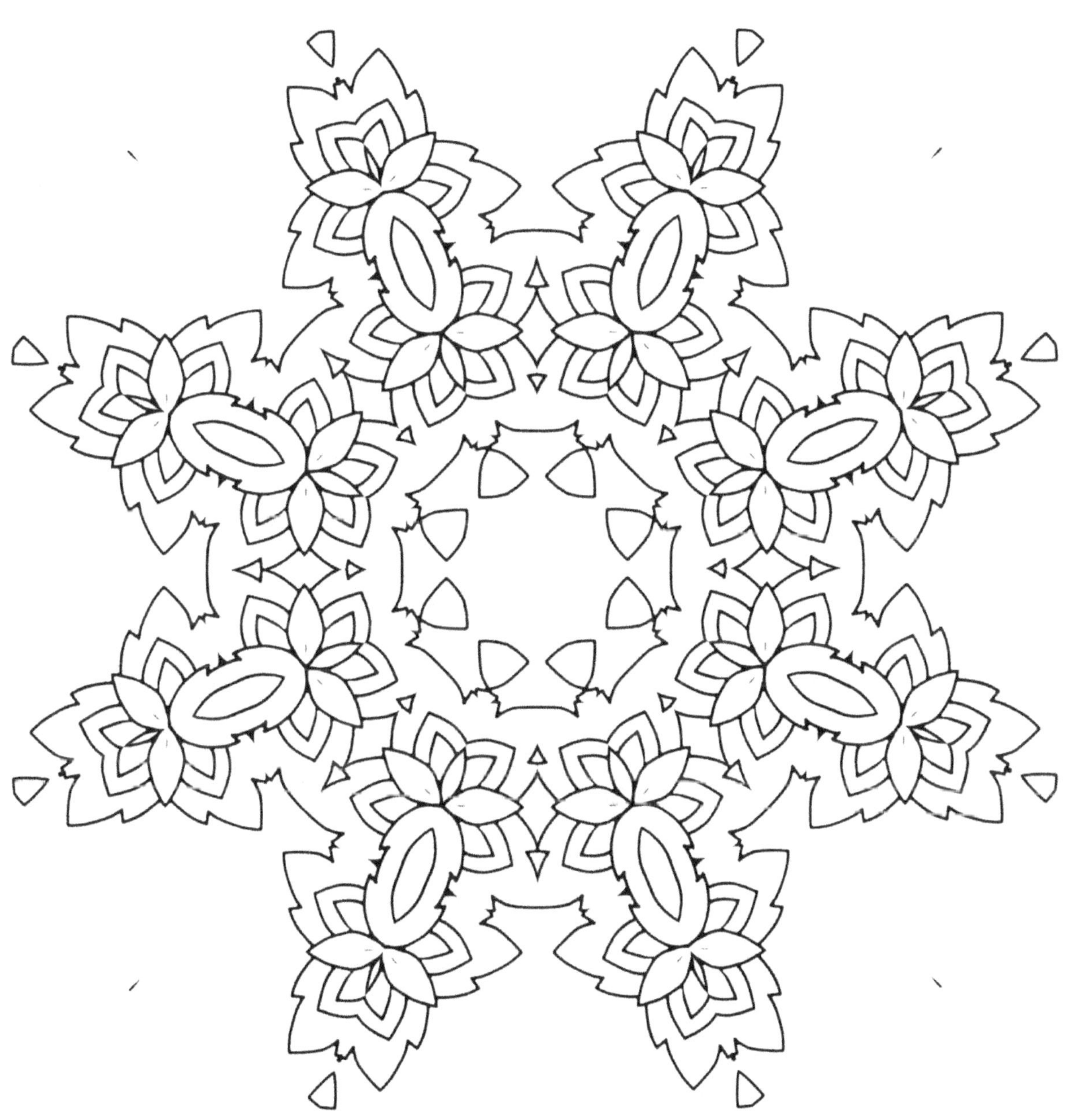

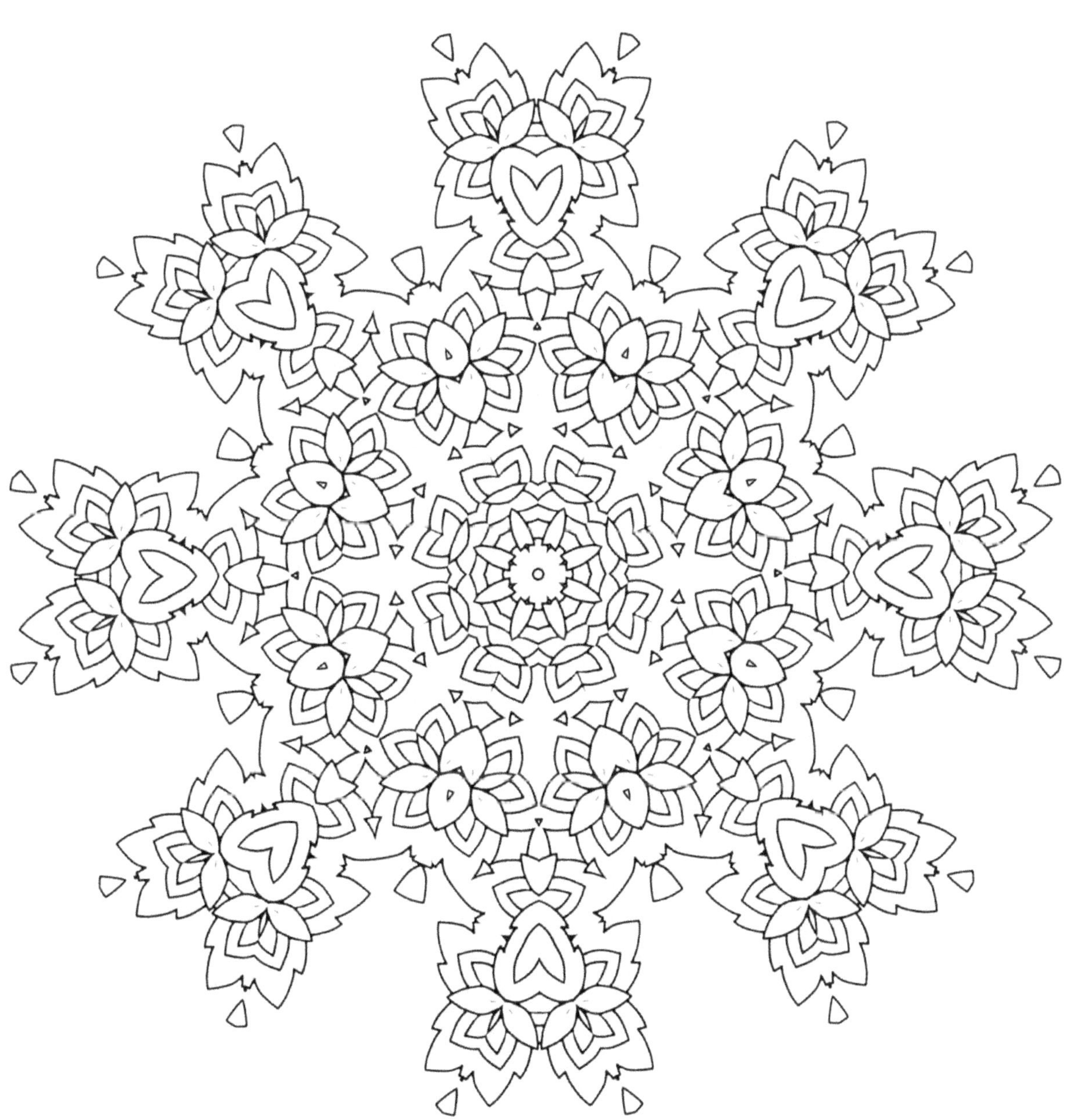

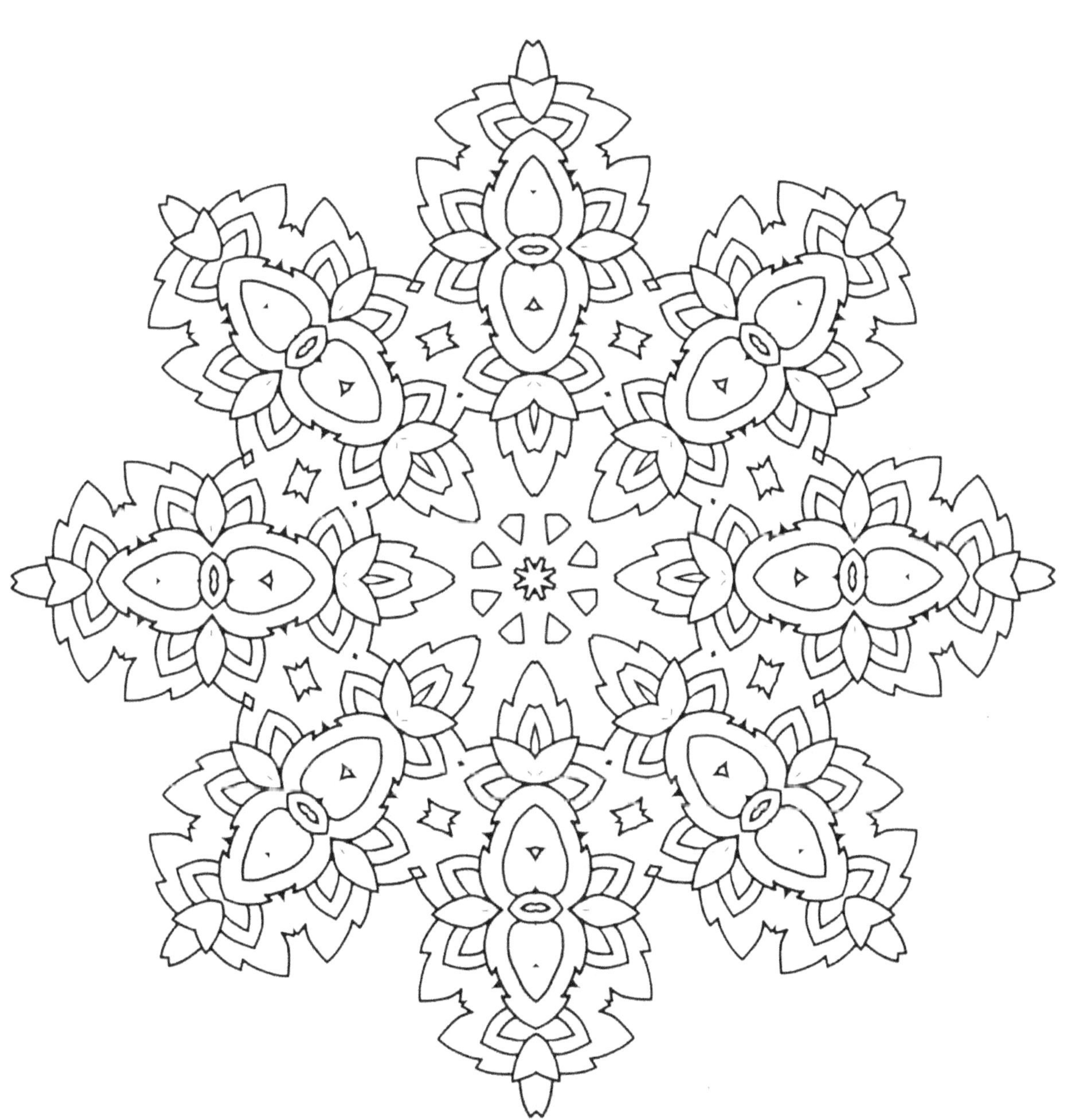

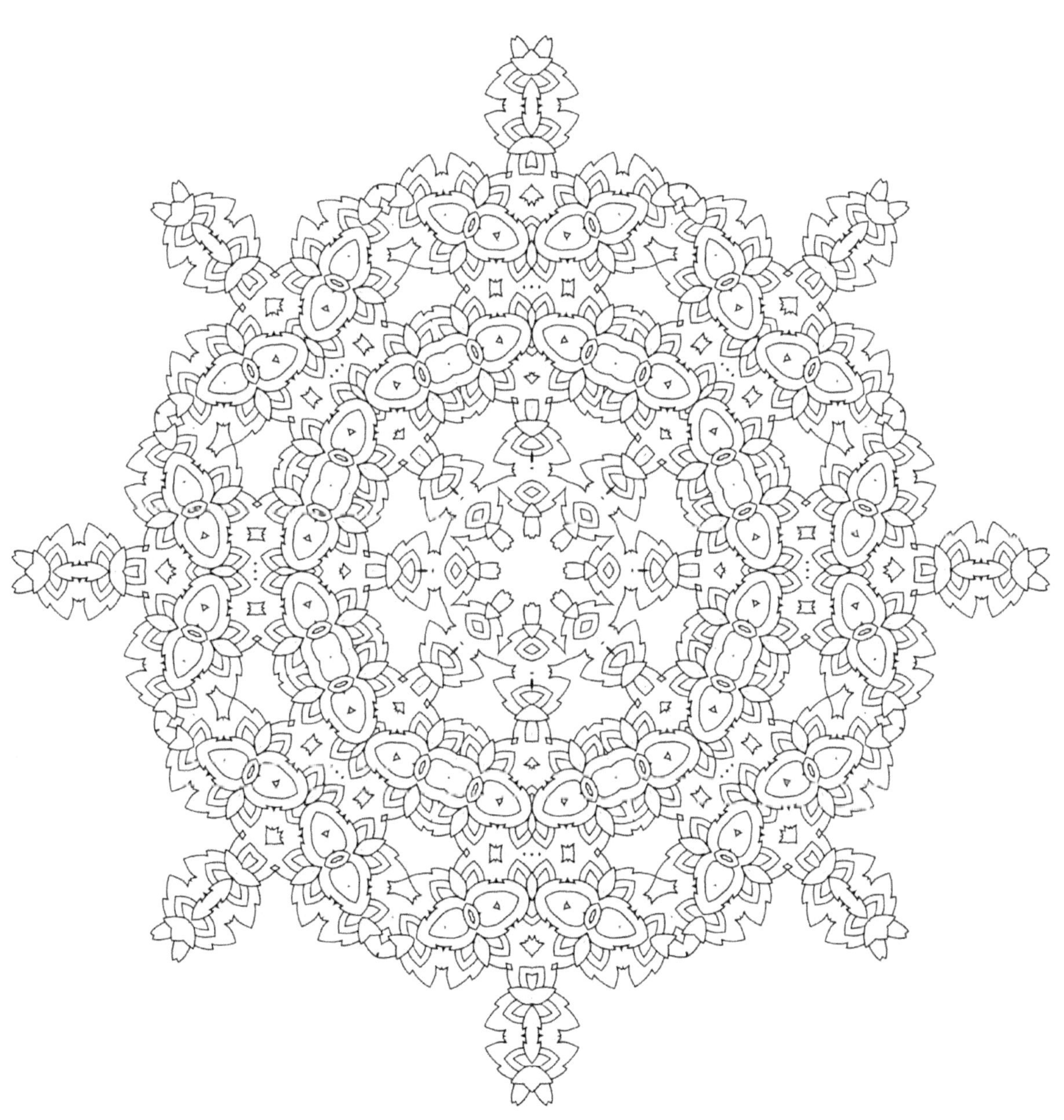

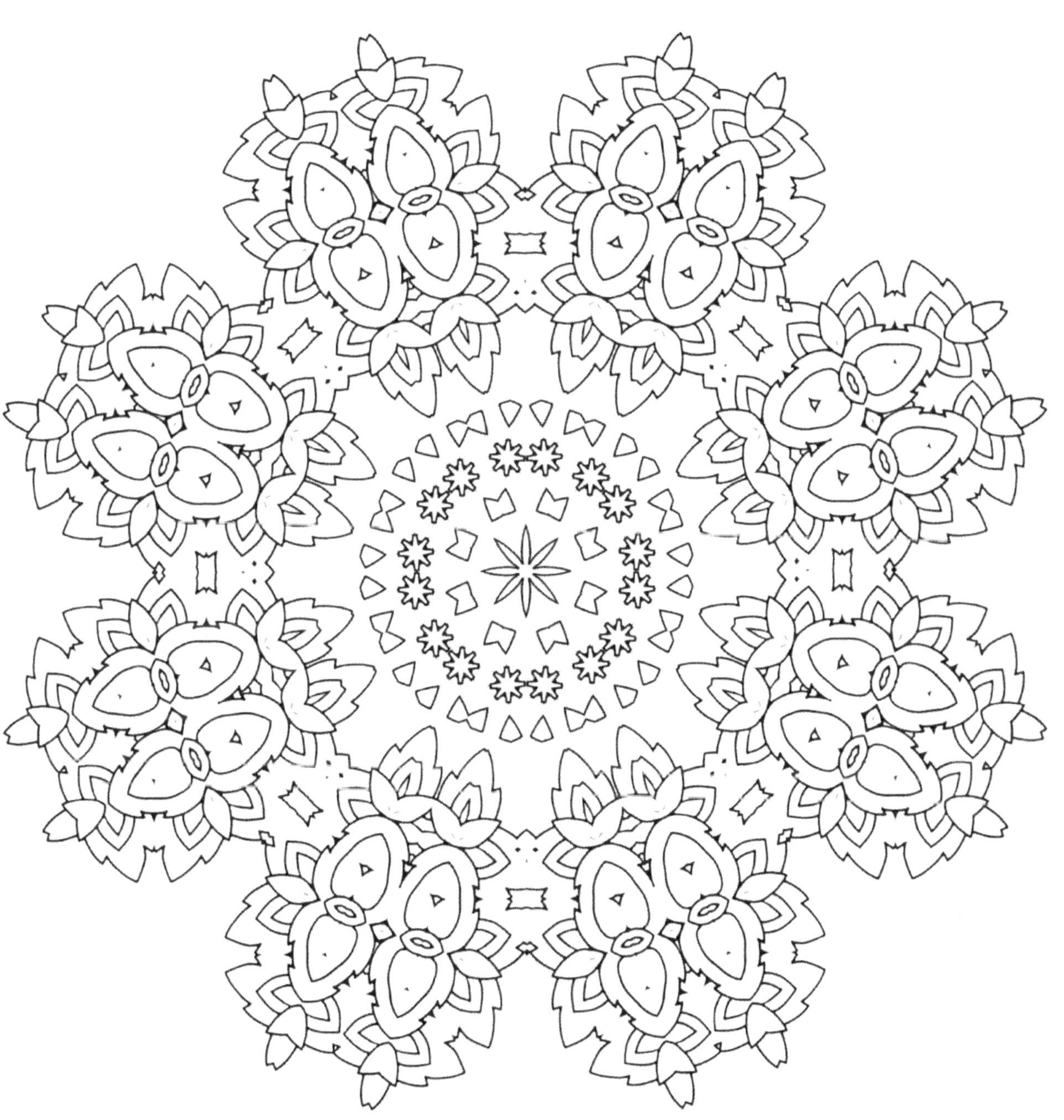

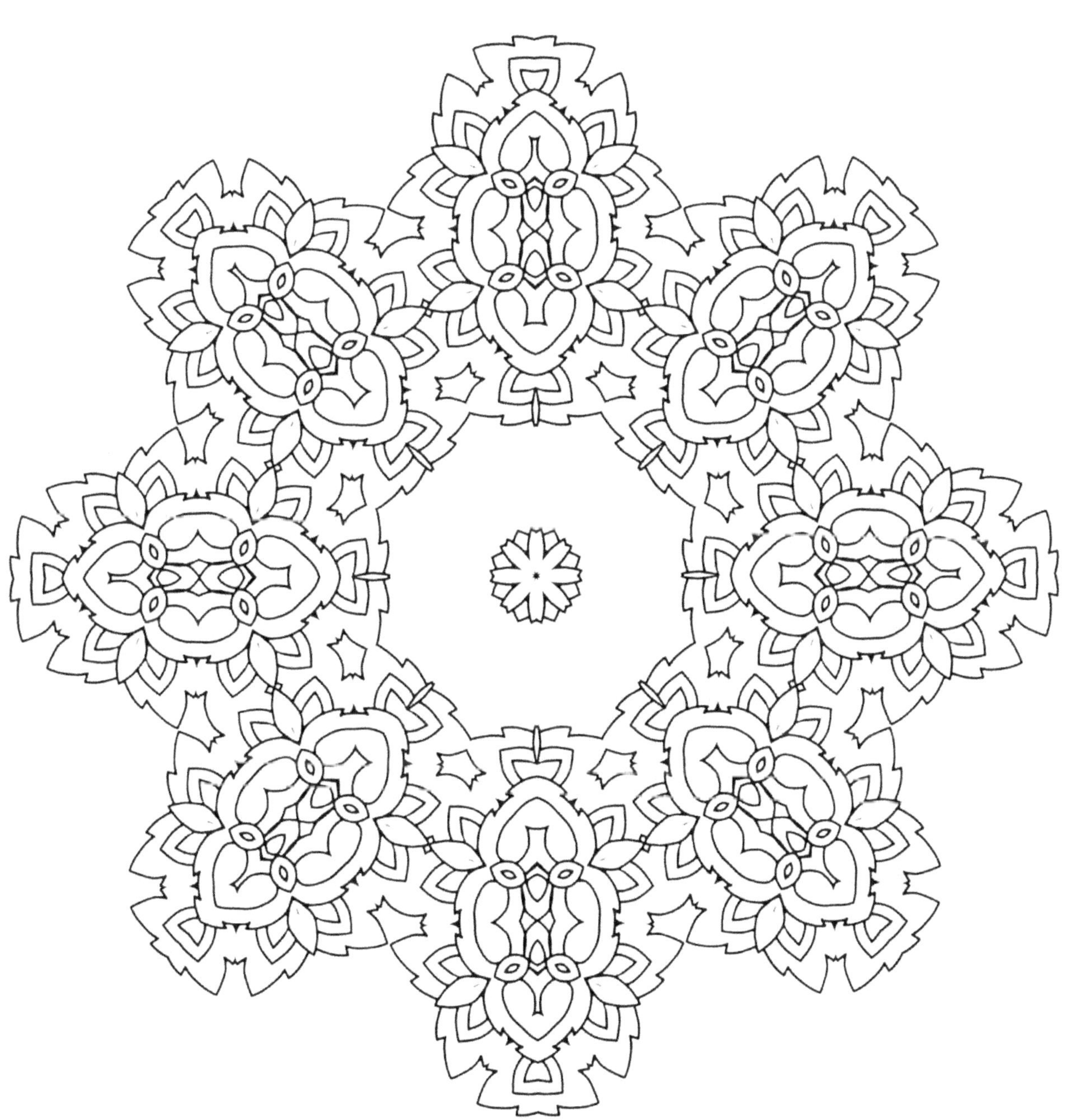

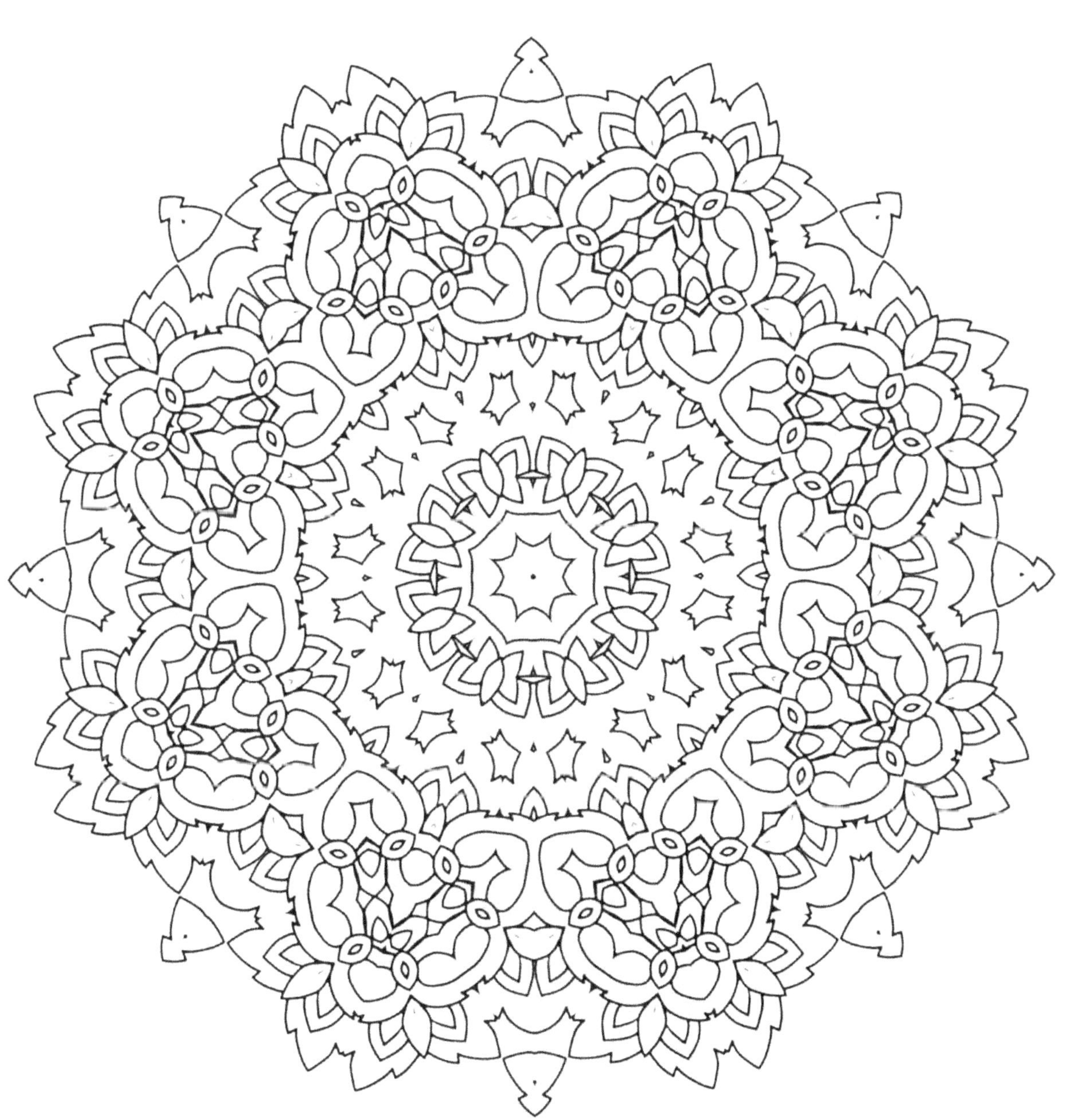

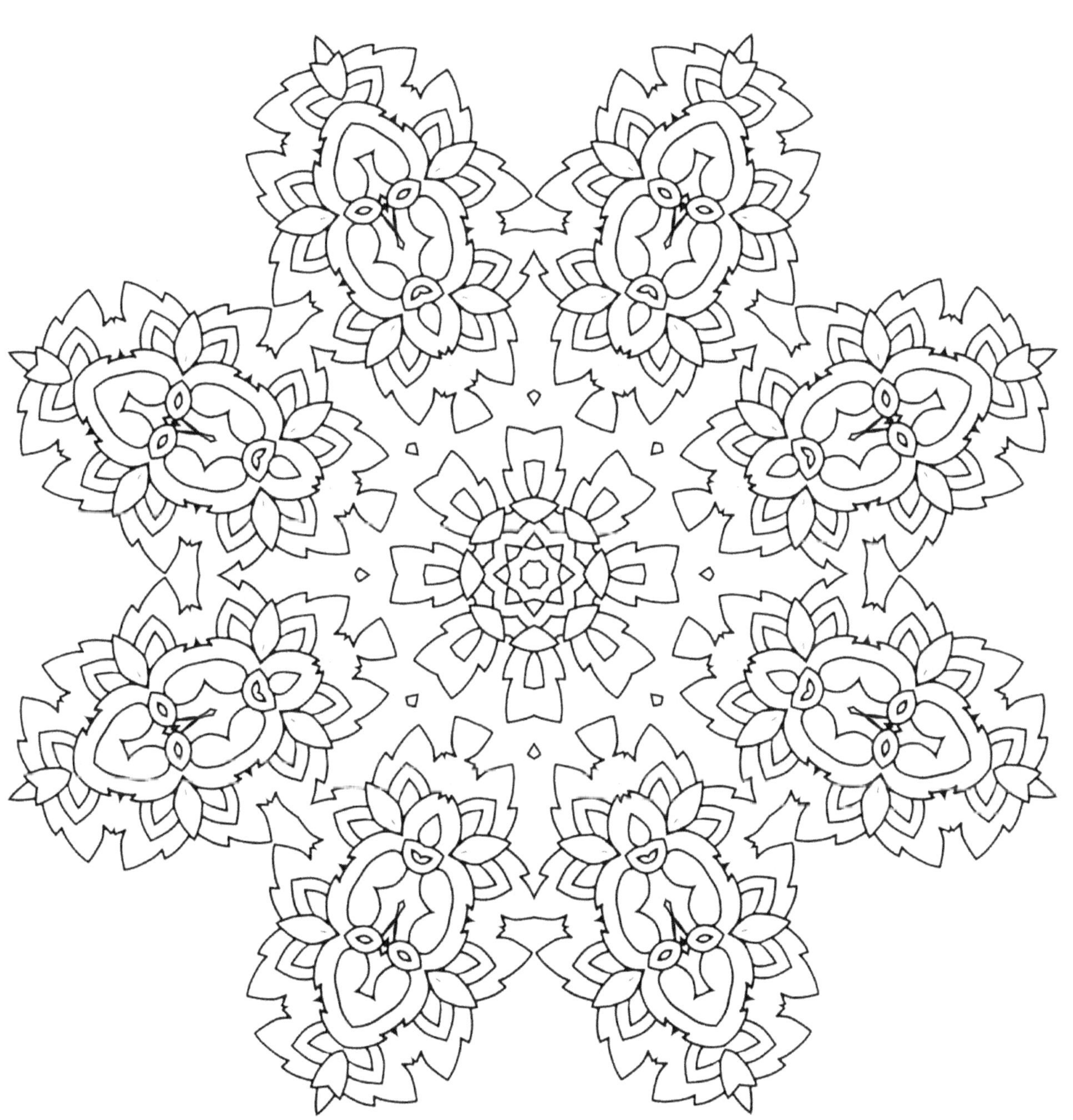

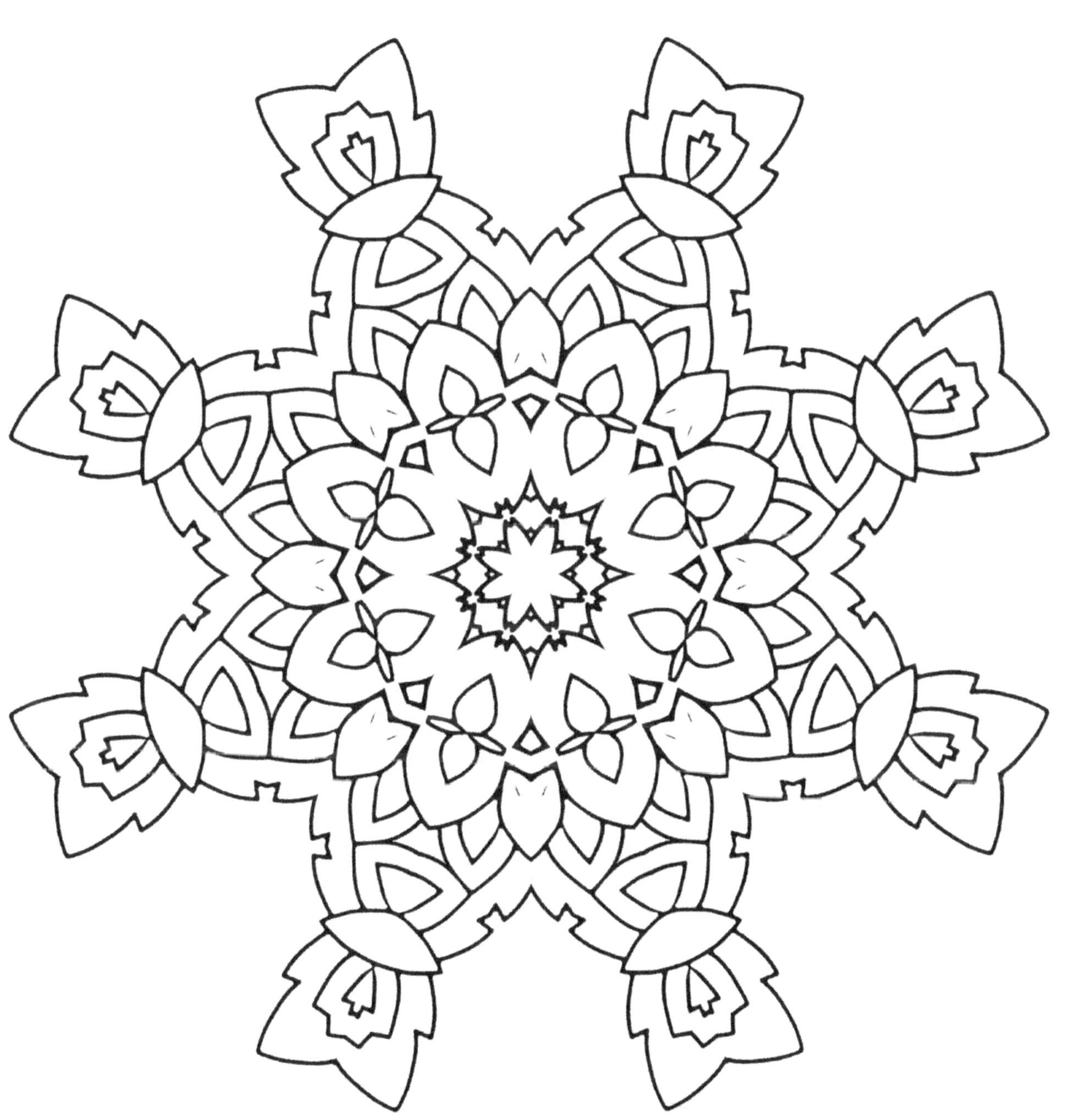

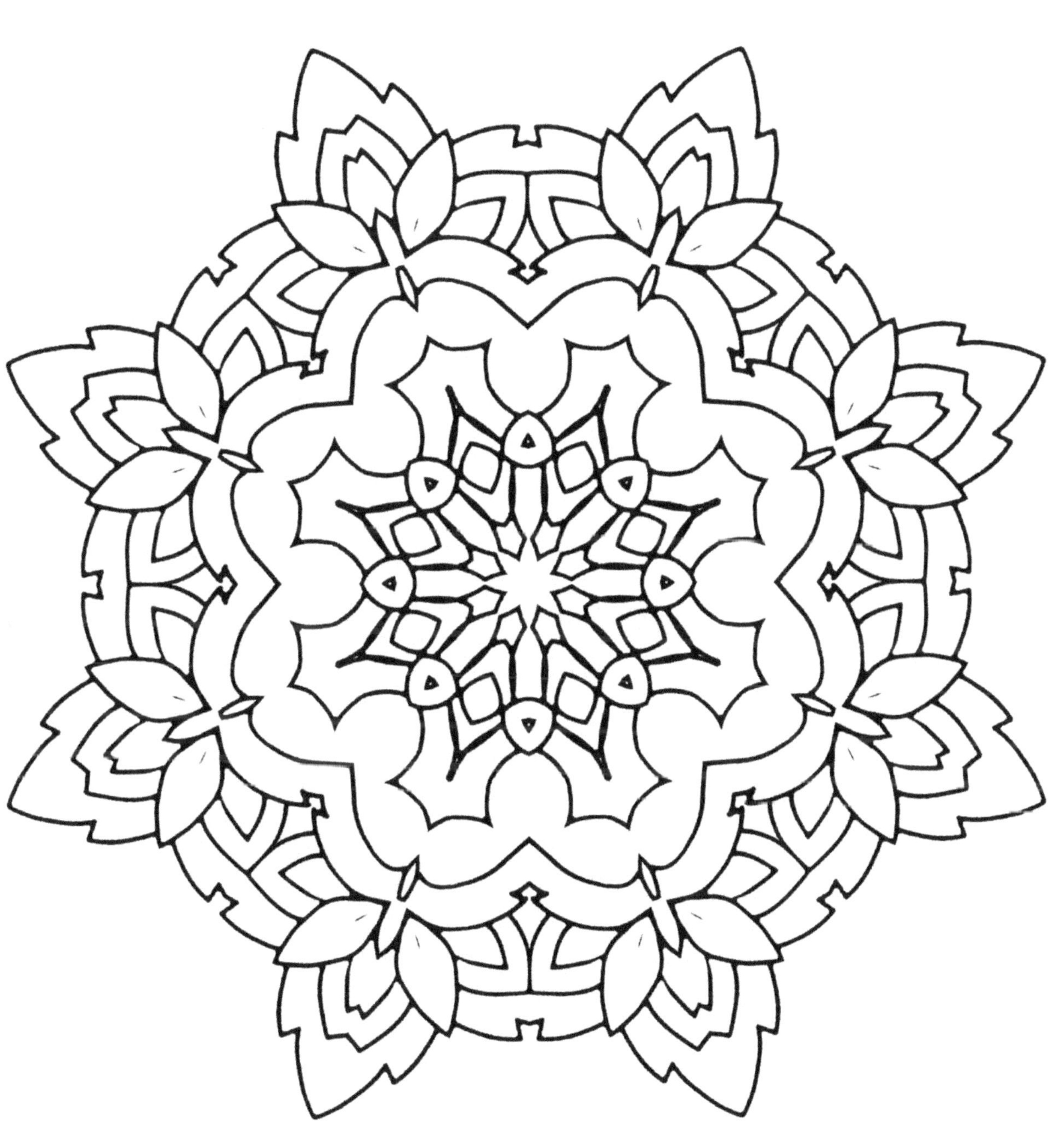

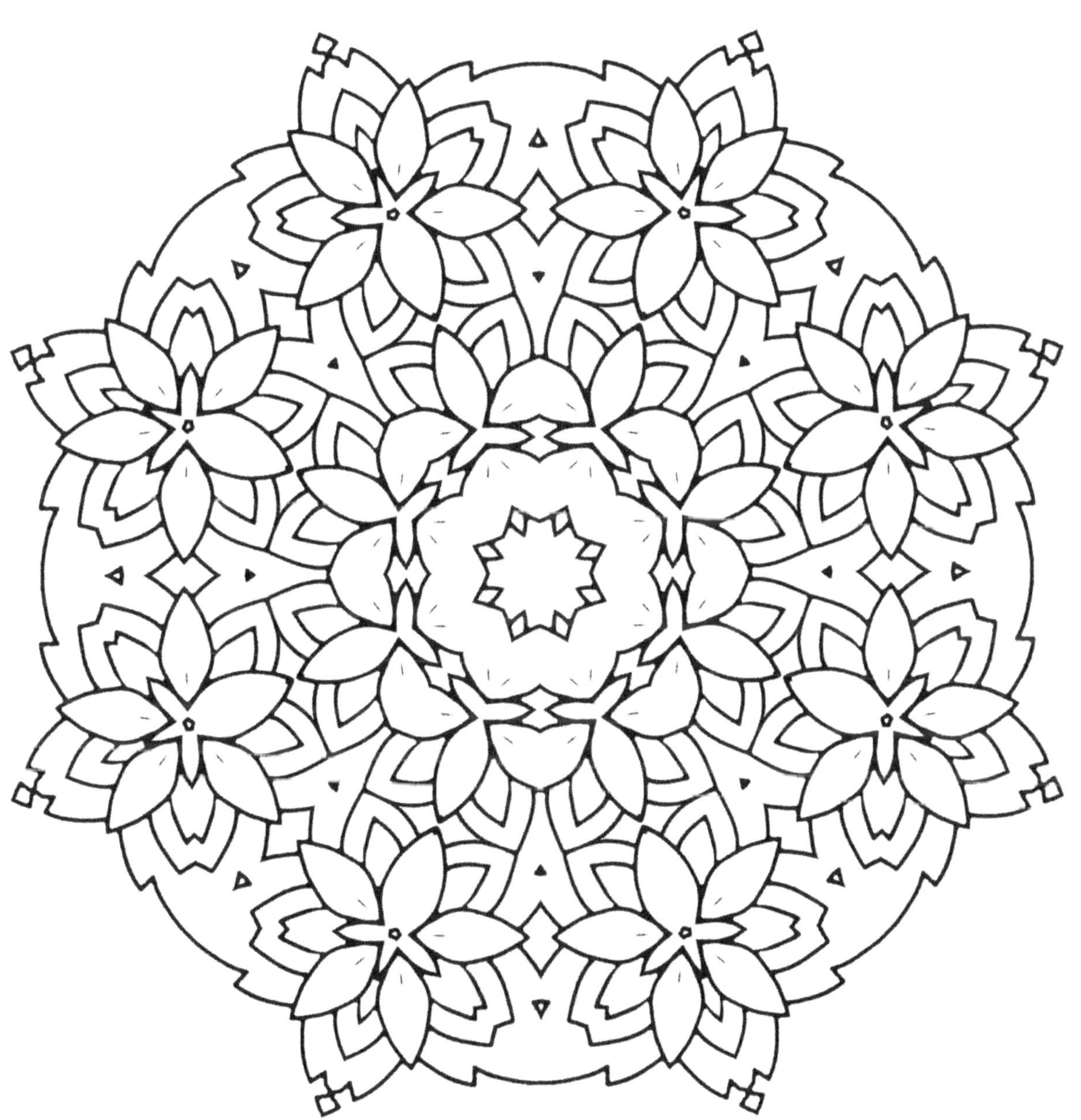

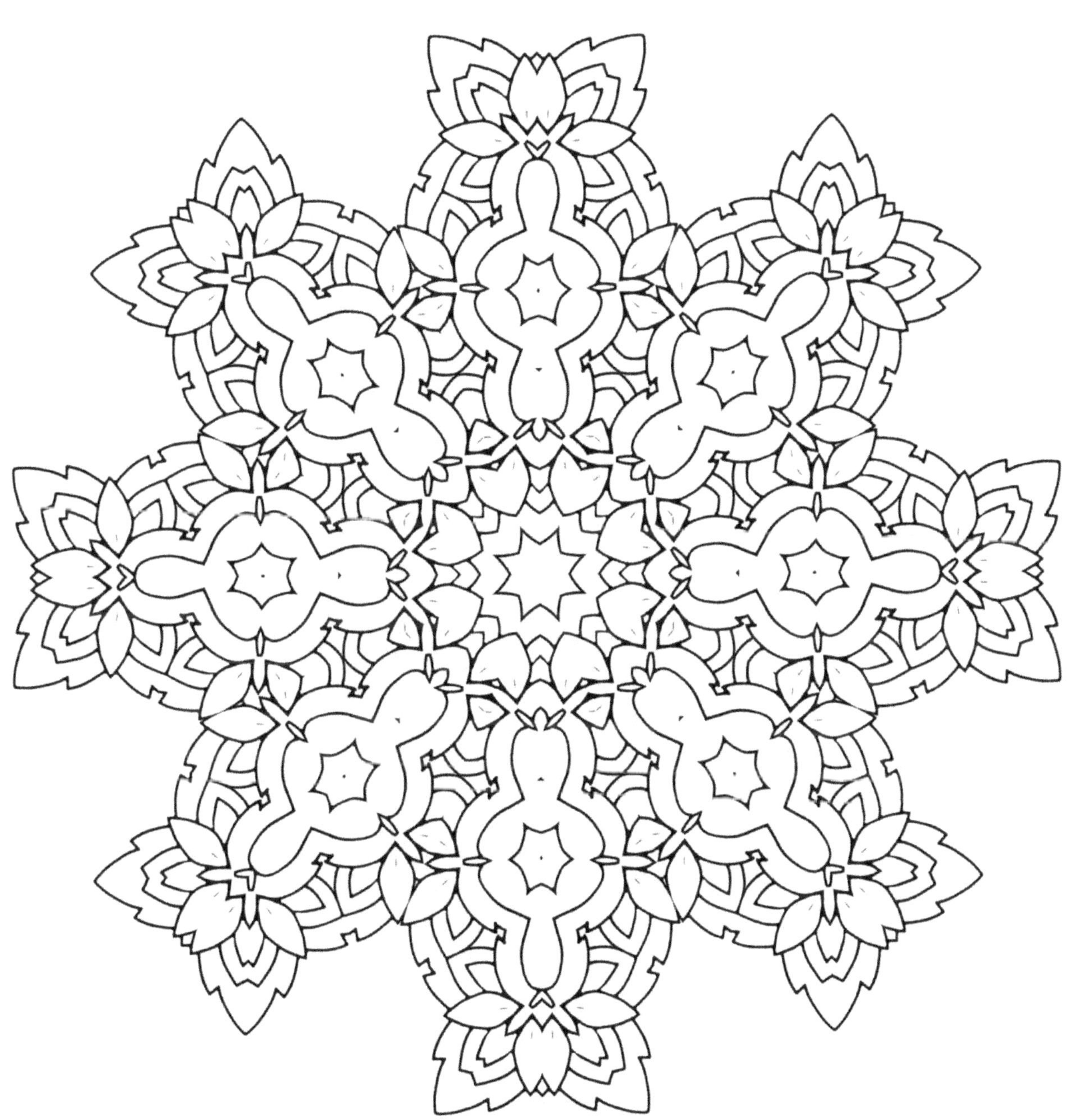

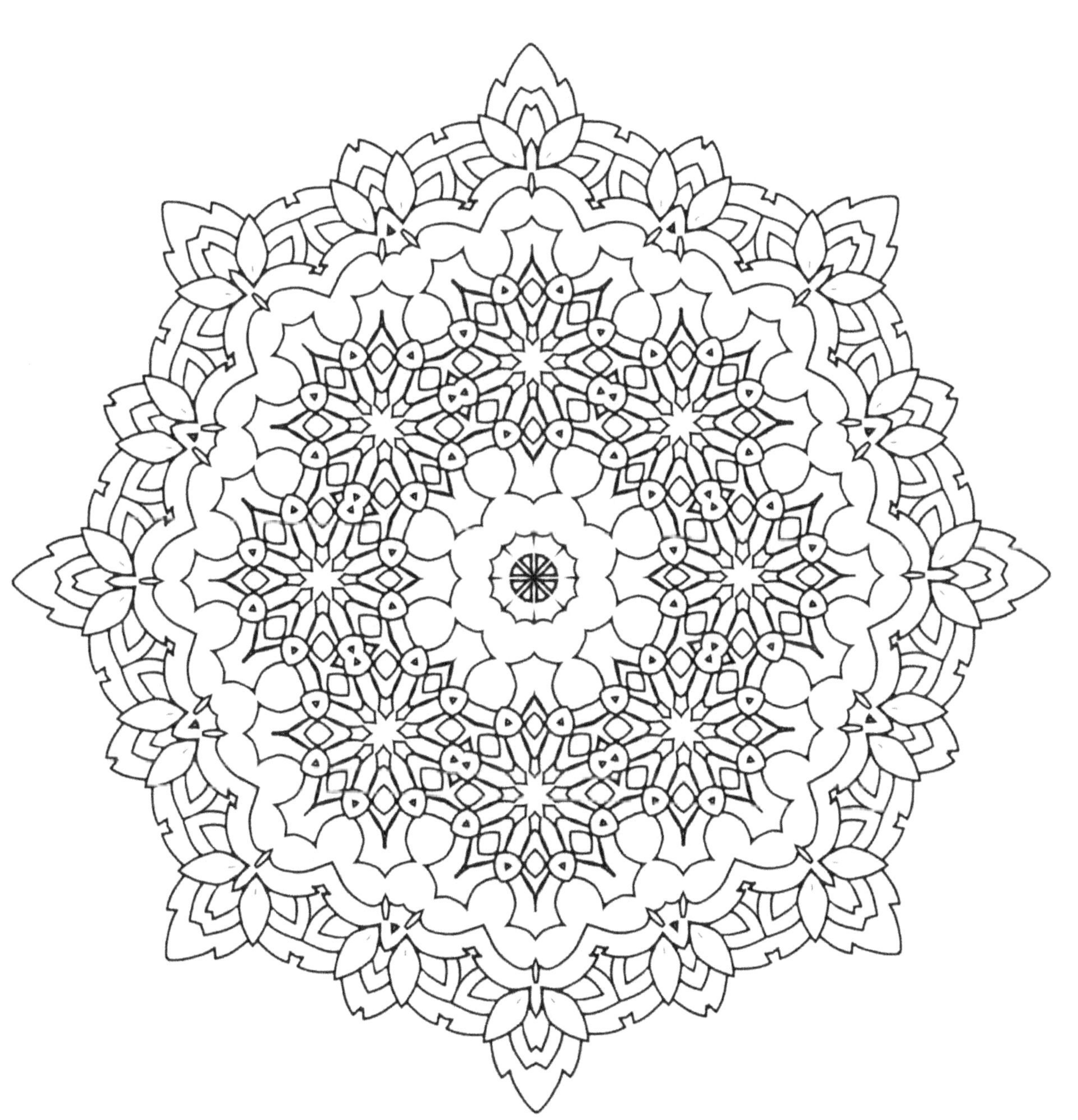

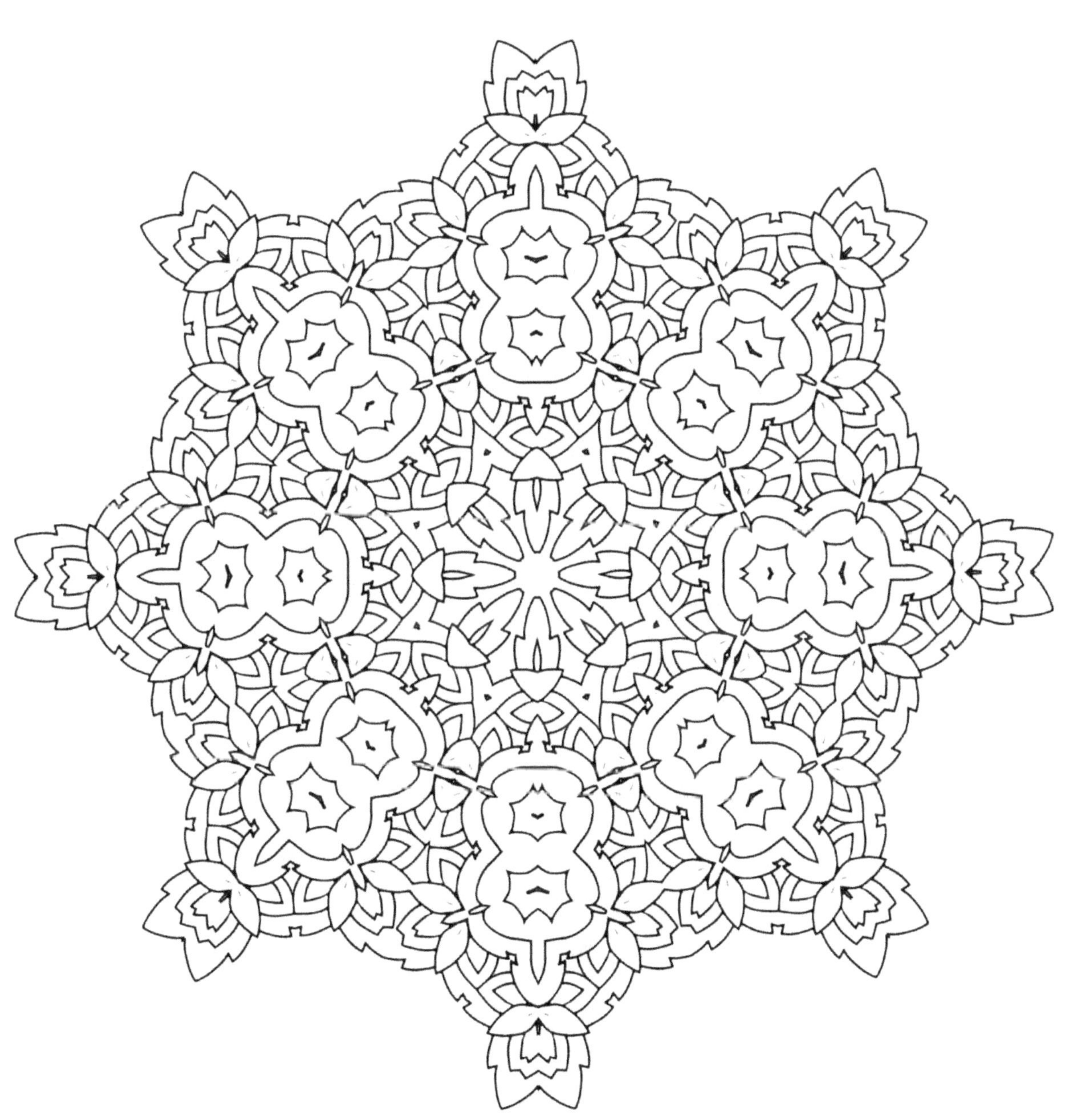

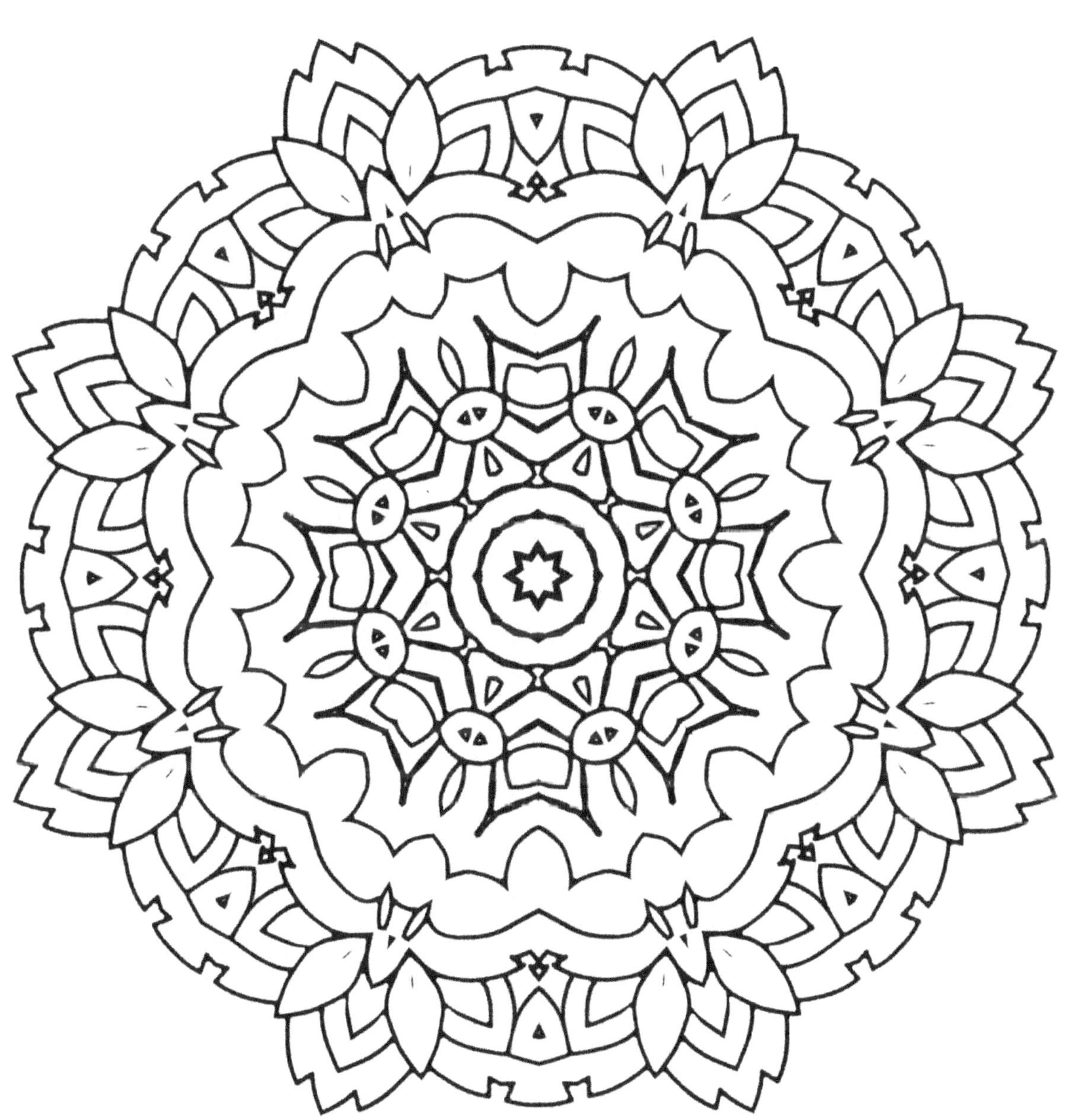

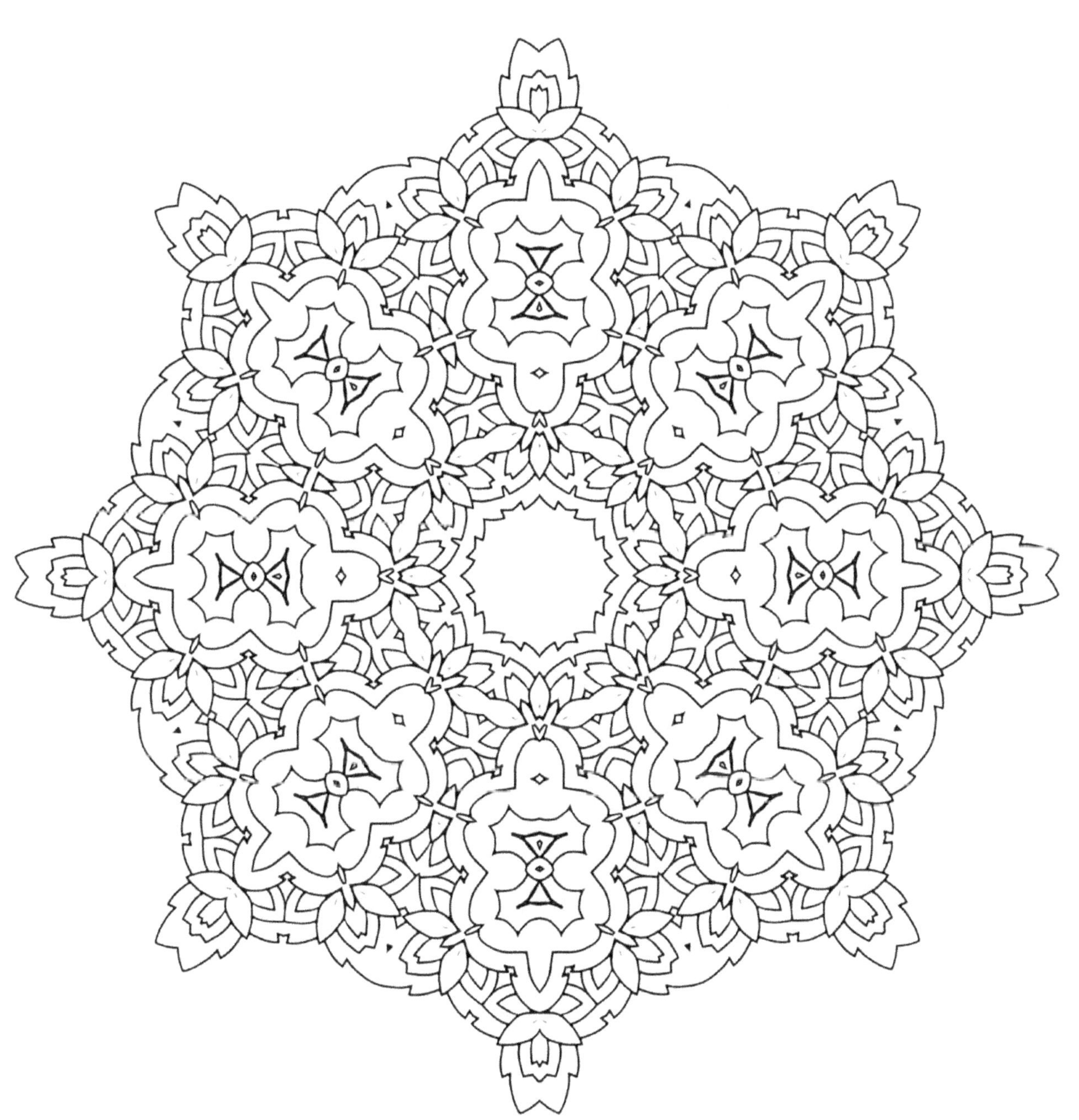

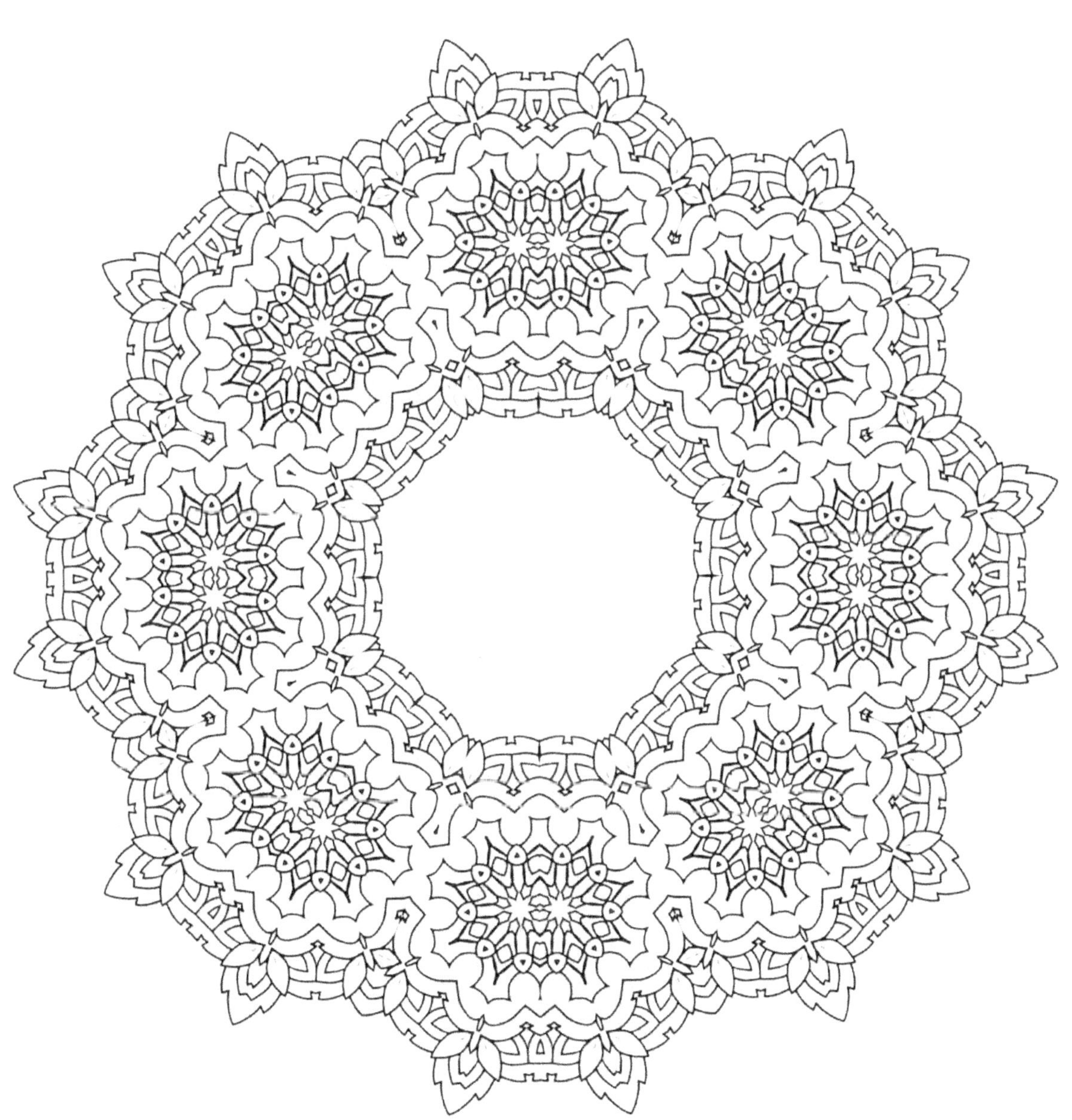

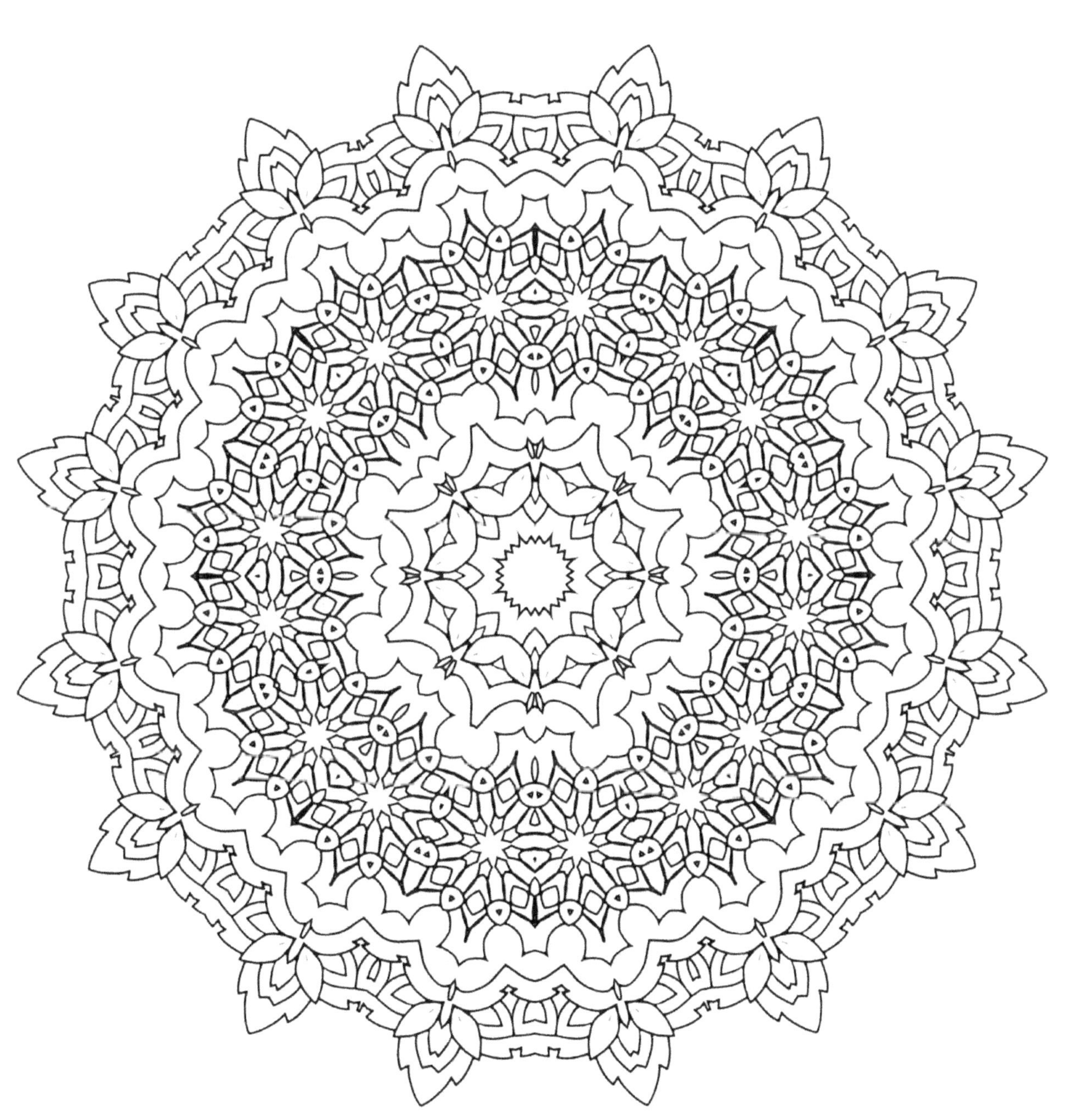

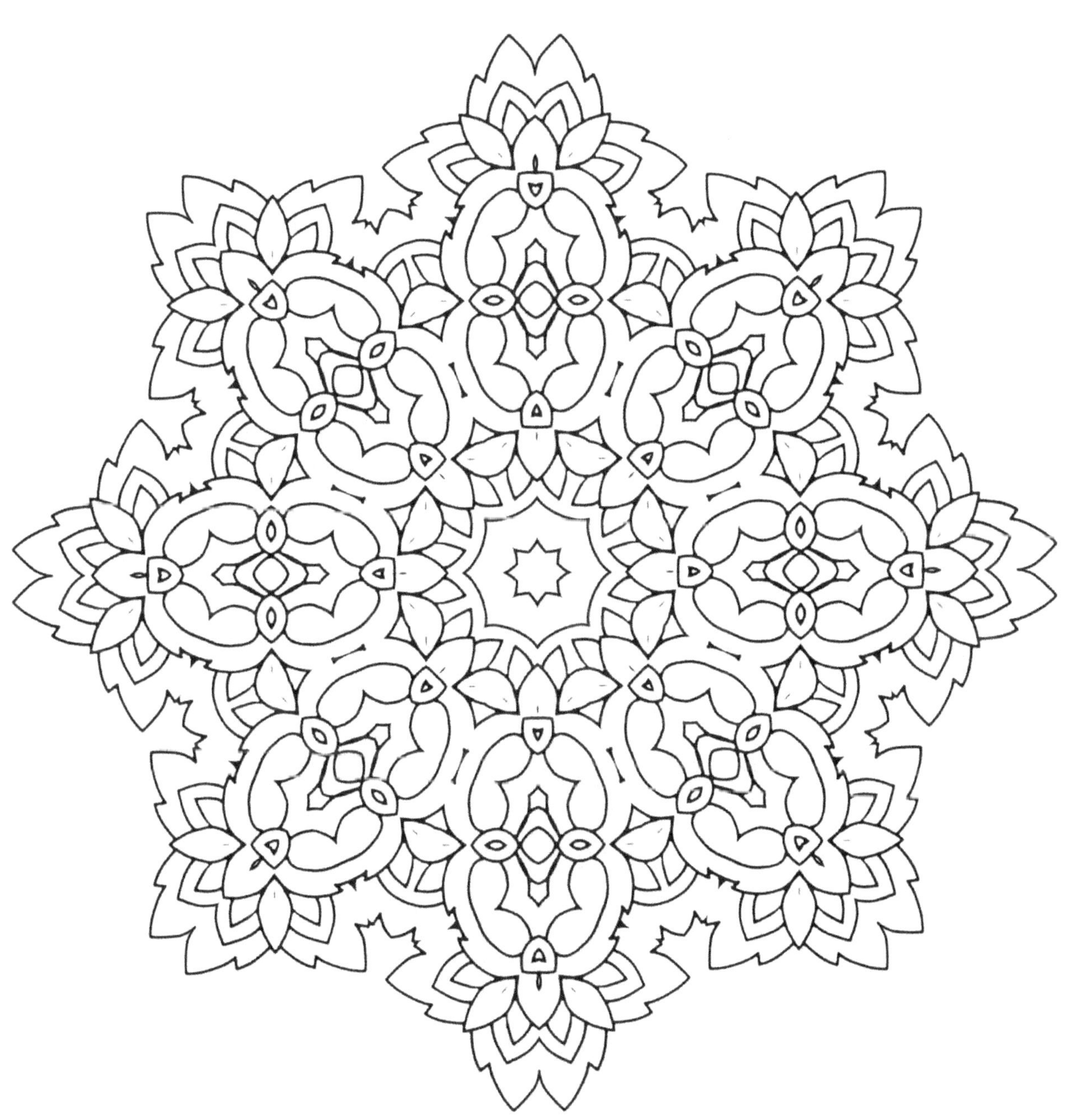

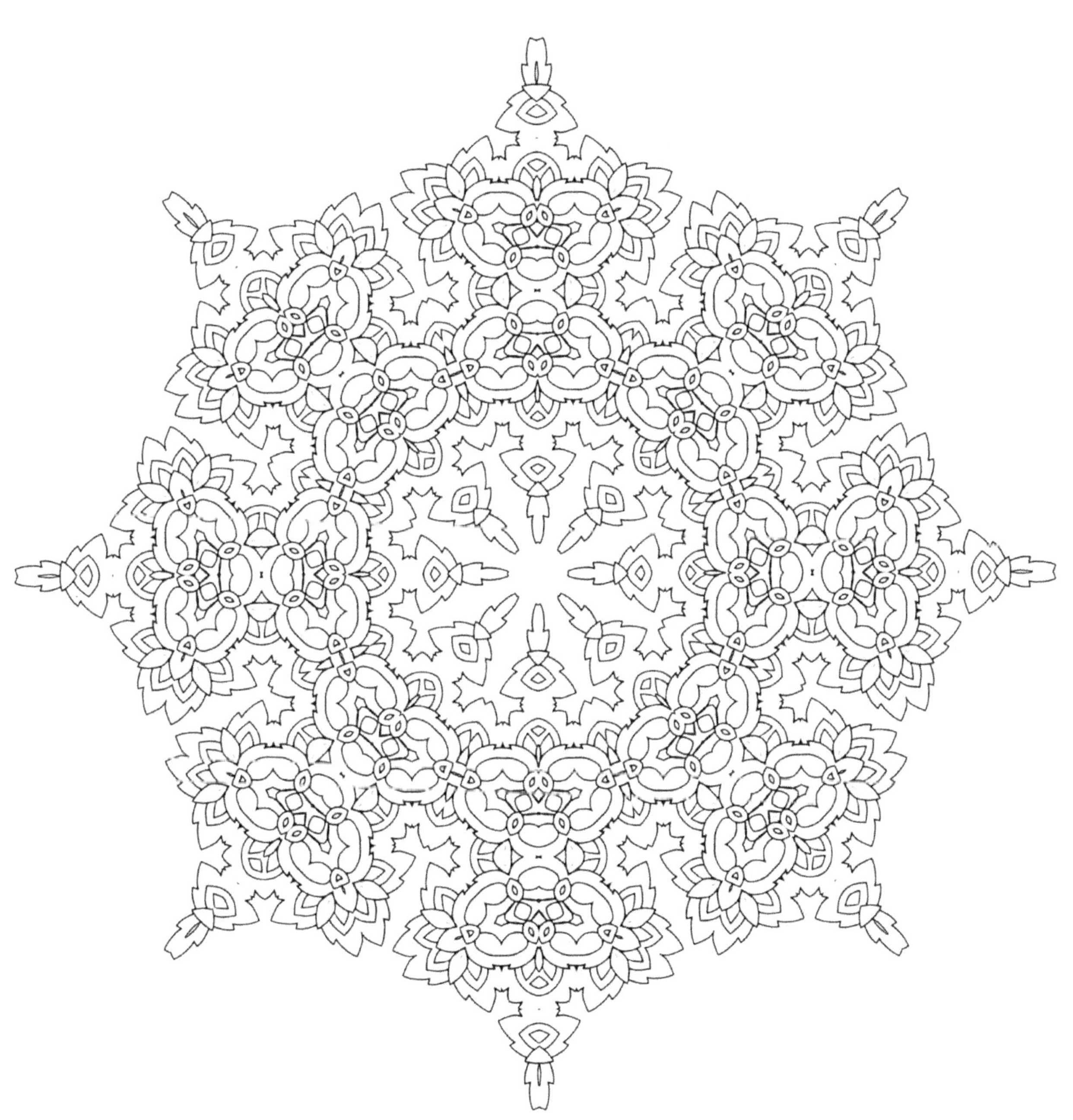

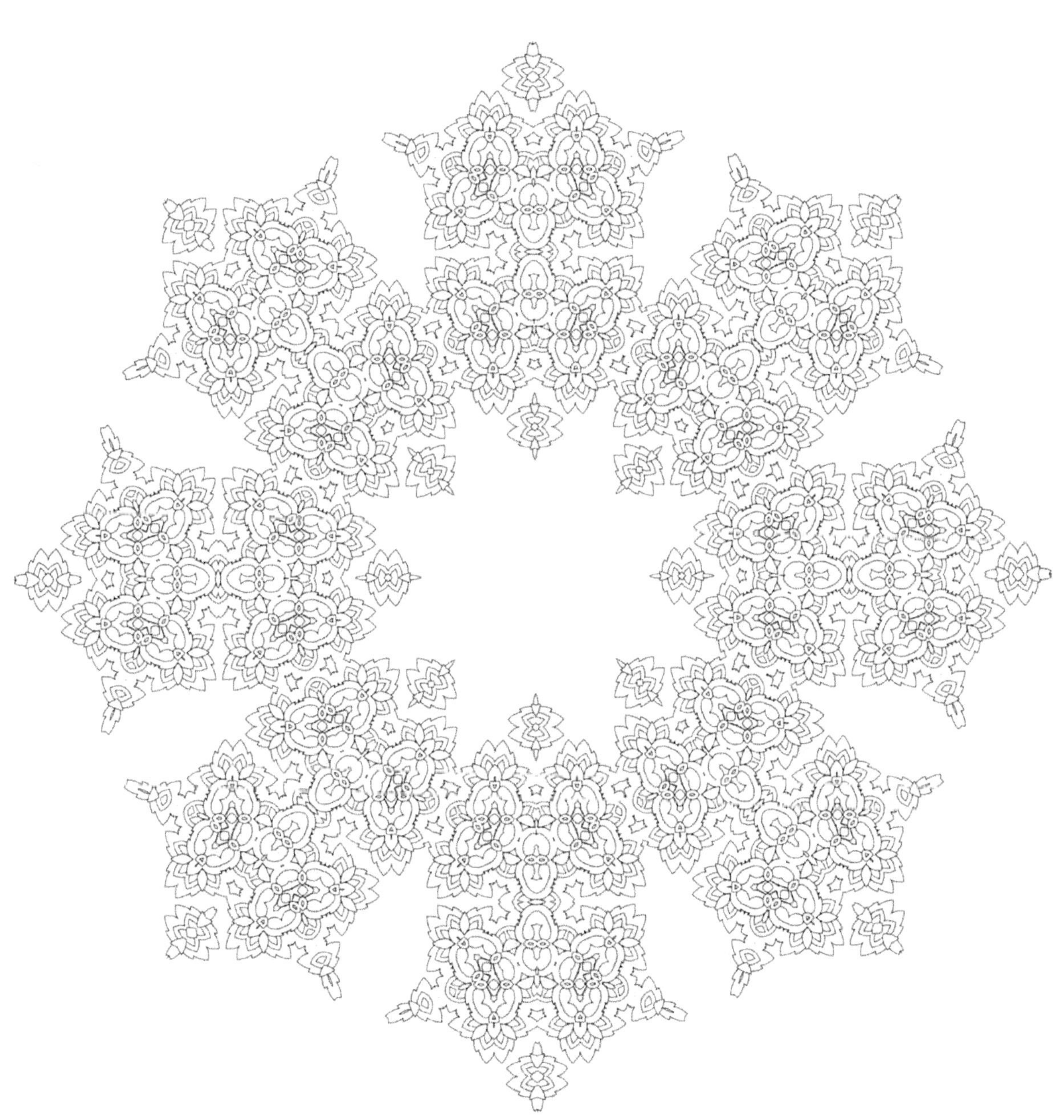

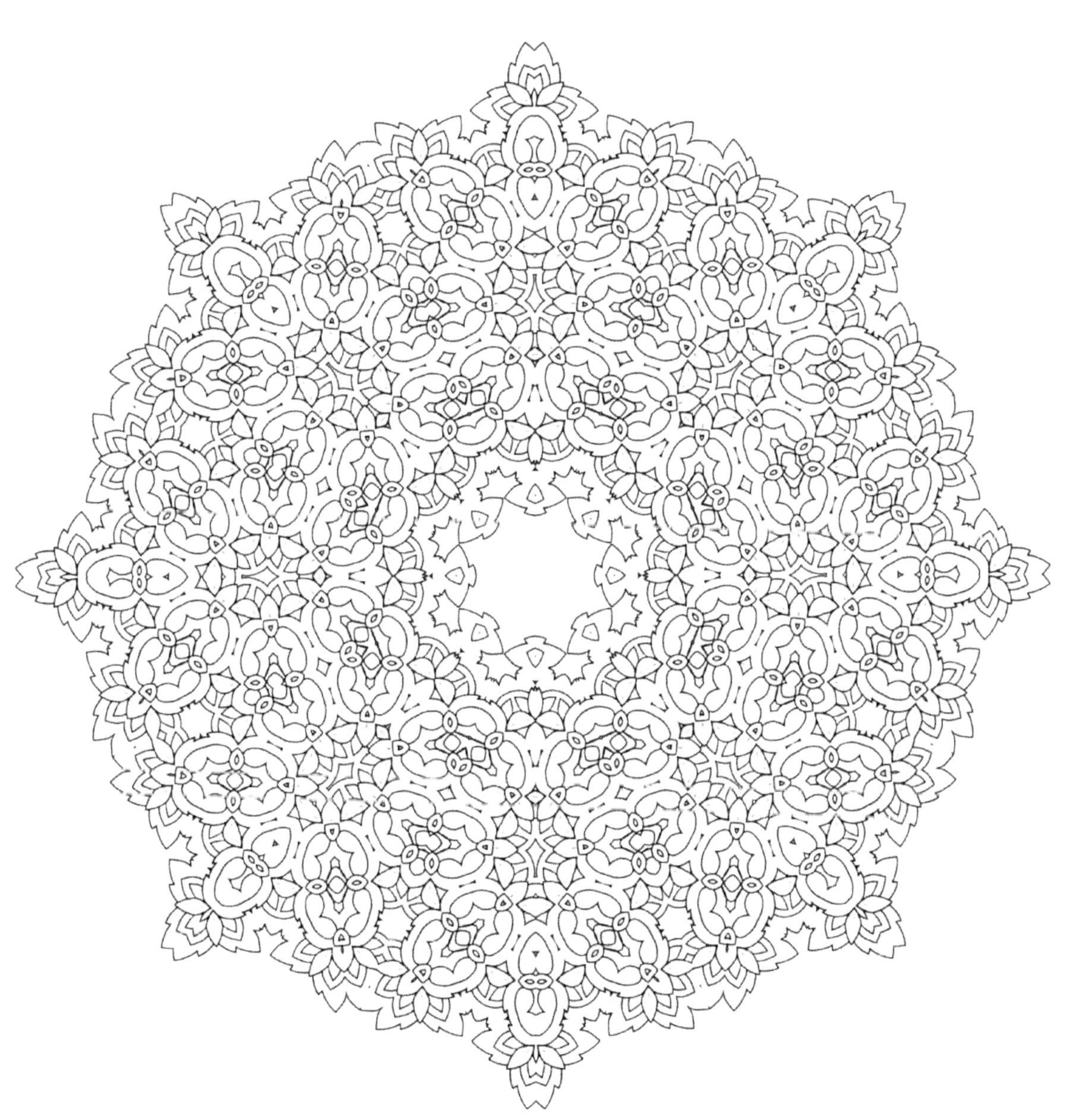

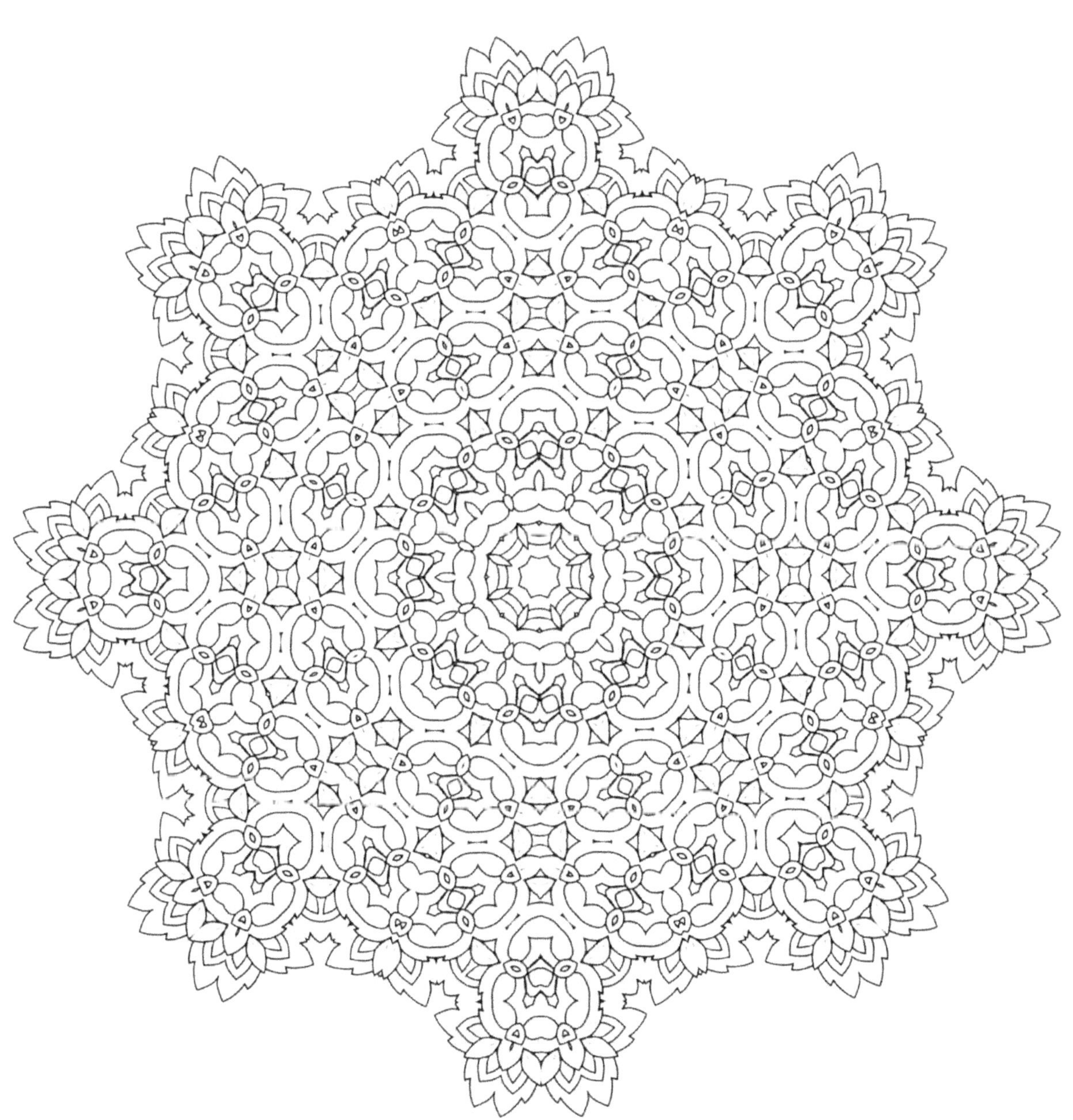

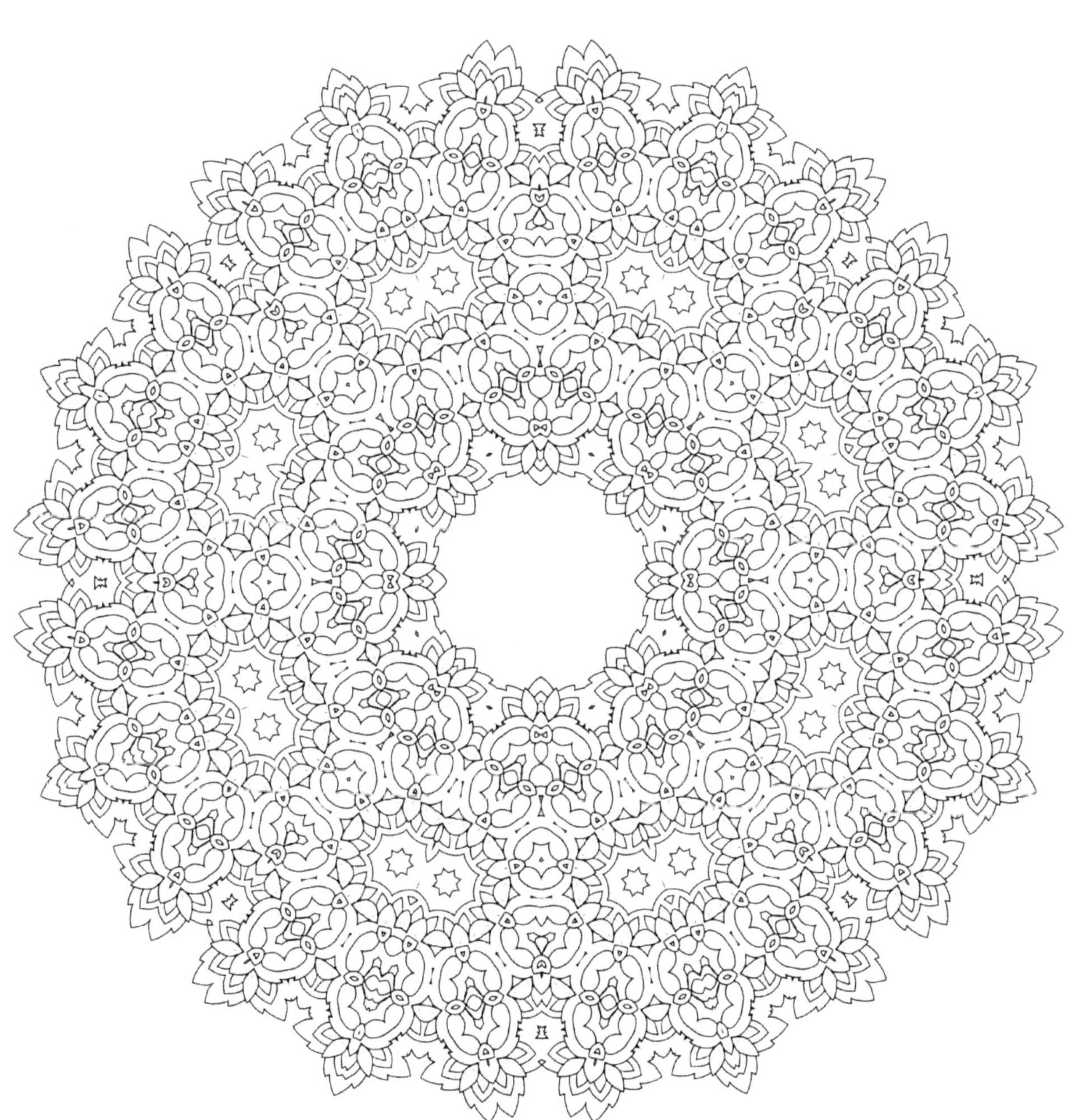

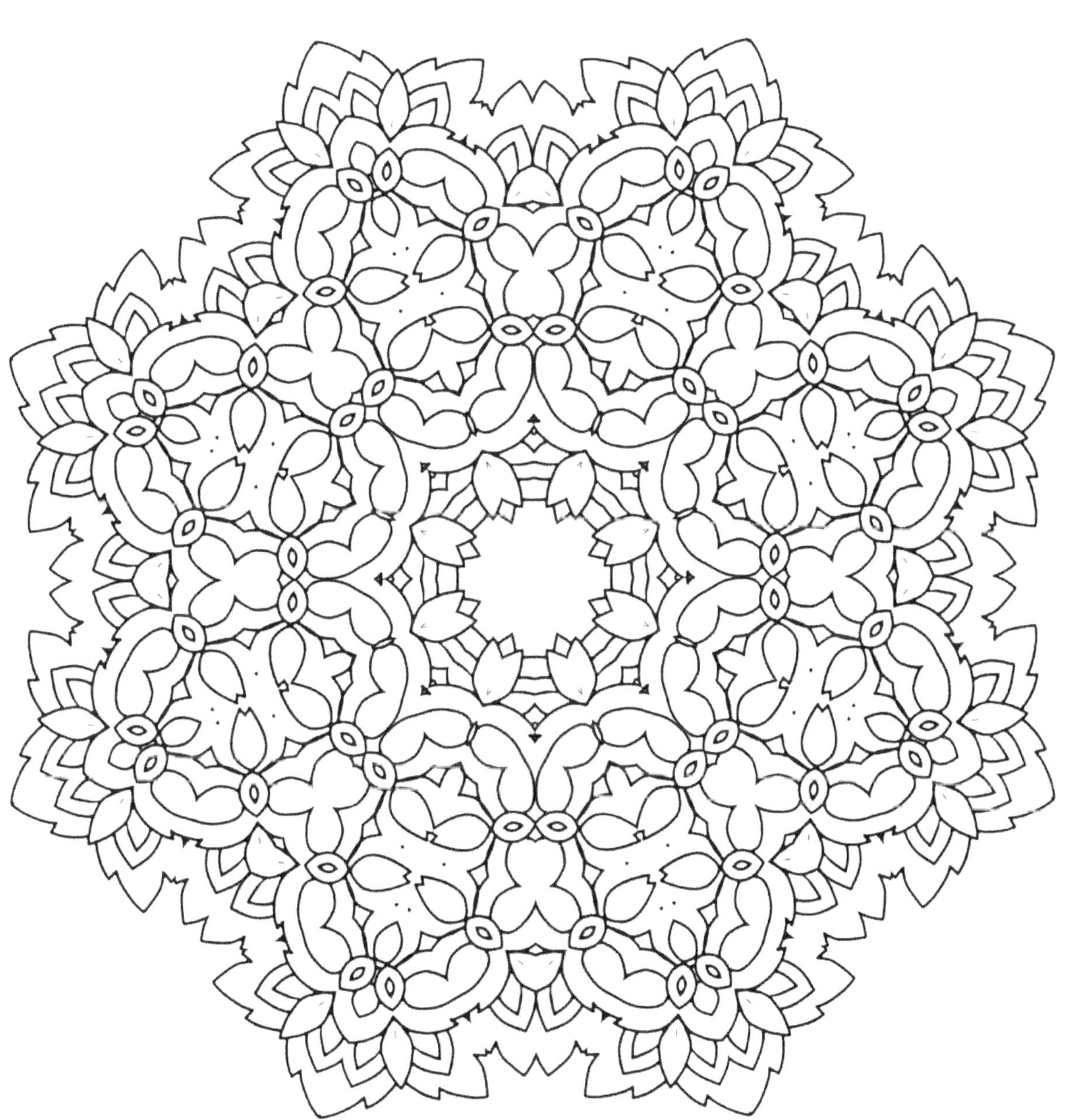

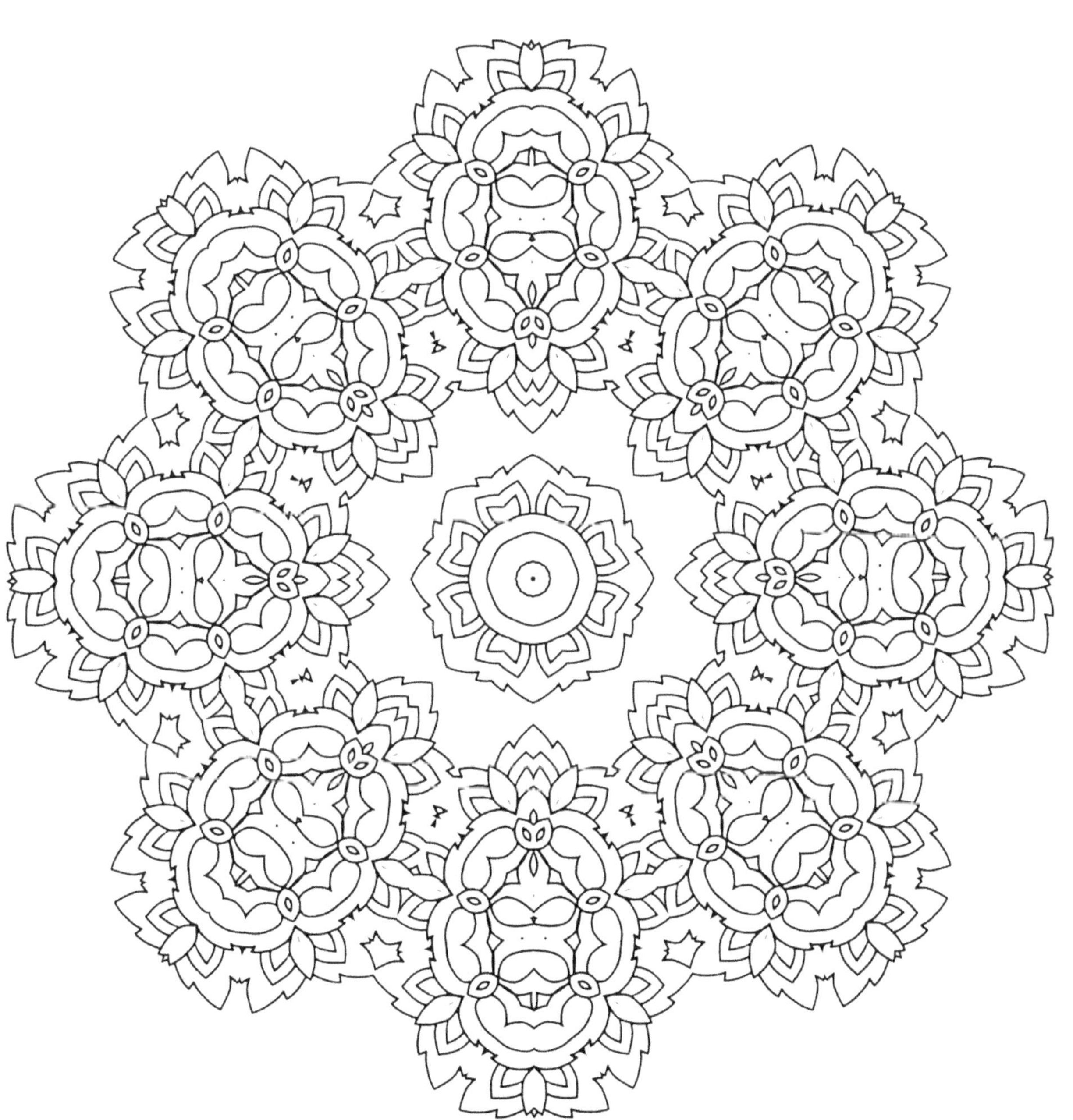

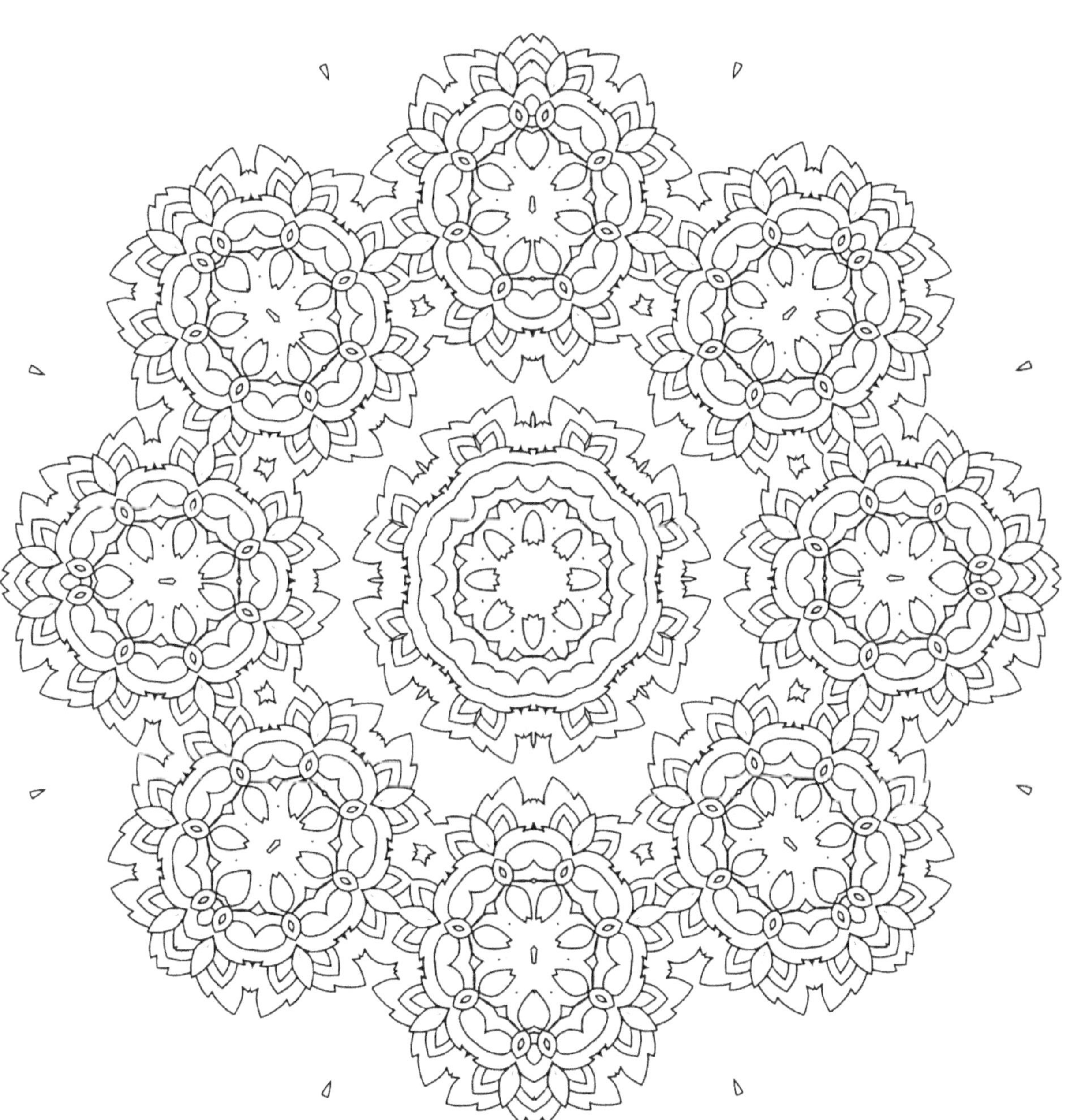

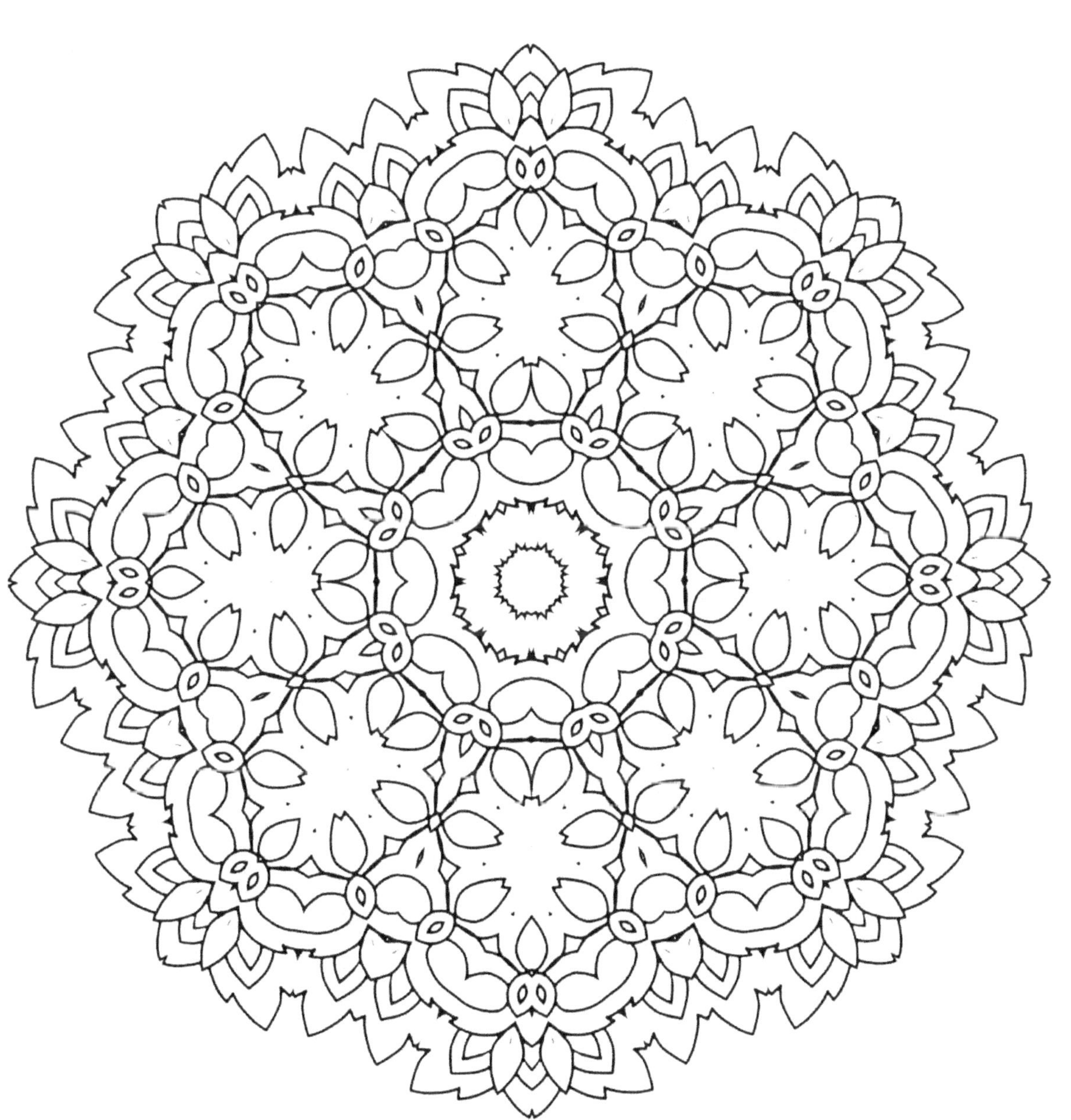

Thank you

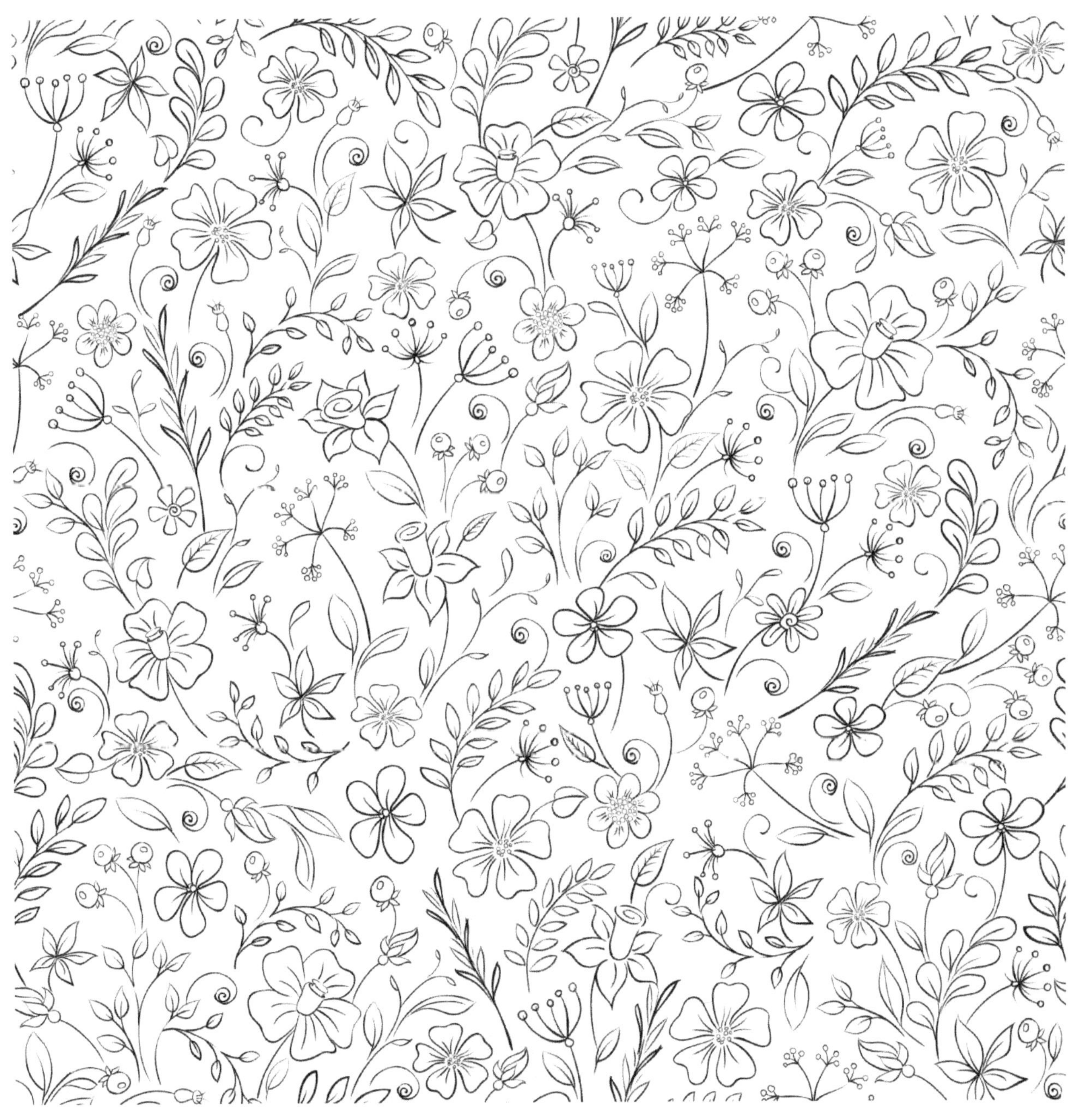

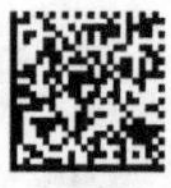